Y0-BUP-410

THE FEMINIZATION OF POVERTY
IN THE UNITED STATES

GARLAND REFERENCE LIBRARY
OF SOCIAL SCIENCE
(VOL. 530)

THE FEMINIZATION OF POVERTY IN THE UNITED STATES

*A Selected, Annotated
Bibliography of the Issues,
1978–1989*

Renee Feinberg
Kathleen E. Knox

GARLAND PUBLISHING, INC. • NEW YORK & LONDON
1990

Library of Congress Cataloging-in-Publication Data

Feinberg, Renee.
  The feminization of poverty in the United States: a selected,
annotated bibliography of the issues, 1978–1989 / Renee Feinberg,
Kathleen E. Knox.
      p.   cm. — (Garland reference library of social science; v.
530)
      ISBN 0–8240–1213–5 (alk. paper)
      1. Poor women—United States—Bibliography. 2. Women heads of
households—United States—Bibliography. 3. Child welfare—United
States—Bibliography. 4. Family policy—United States—Bibliography.
I. Knox, Kathleen. II. Title. III. Series.
Z7164.C4F45   1990
[HV1445]
016.36283'0973—dc20   90–2869
                                                          CIP

Printed on acid-free, 250-year-life paper
Manufactured in the United States of America

To American women and children in poverty, who inspire us,

and to our friends and families, especially Sheelah and Jan.

Table of Contents

Preface

In this annotated bibliography we focus on the issues of poverty and the feminization of poverty; children, child support, and child care; employment issues including affirmative action, comparable worth and pay equity; Reaganomics; the special problems of black women; teenage mothers and their children; older women, social security and pension issues; health and homelessness; welfare policy and welfare reform, including workfare; and options for a national family policy.

We reviewed the American monographic, periodical, and document literature of the last decade, relying on computer searches of several social science databases, including Psychological Abstracts, Sociological Abstracts, Index Medicus, Magazine Index, Public Affairs Information Service, Social Science Citation Index, Educational Resources Information Center, Family Resources, Work/Family Life Database, Abstracts of Working Papers in Economics, International Review of Publications in Sociology, Ageline, Legal Resource Index, Popular Magazine Review Online, and Index to U. S. Government Periodicals. We searched manually the Alternative Press Index, Left Index, and Women's Studies Abstracts.

The literature on the feminization of poverty peaked in the mid-eighties due to concern about the effects of the Reagan budget cuts and tax policies on poor women and children. In the last few years, emphasis has shifted to reform measures such as child-support enforcement and discussion of the underclass.

We selected those references on the feminization of poverty in the United States which were informative and accessible. We did not include newspaper articles. We concentrated on citing materials found in a variety of indexes. We cited entire collections of essays if most of the contents were relevant. In cases where only a few of the essays were useful, they have been cited individually. References were included if they were available to the target audience, undergraduate students in a medium-sized college library with access to a federal depository collection and interlibrary loan services. We deemed an item available if a check of the OCLC (Online Computer Library Center) database indicated holdings in several libraries, thus making it available through interlibrary loan. Dissertations were not included because they are difficult to obtain through interlibrary loan.

Each topic is introduced with an essay elaborating the issues as they relate to the feminization of poverty. Each chapter includes citations to books, journal articles, government documents, and research papers in a single alphabetical sequence.

Acknowledgments

We wish to thank Natalie Kupferberg, Martha Neftleberg, Anita McLoughlin, James Mahoney, Jane Oswald Mitchell, Polly Thistlewaite, Cynthia Van Hazinga, the librarians at the New York Public Library and the Bobst Library of New York University, and the Research Foundation of the City University of New York for a PSC-CUNY two-year research award.

Renee Feinberg, Associate Professor, is a
reference librarian and bibliographer at Brooklyn College
of the City University of New York. Kathleen Knox is
Reference/Documents Librarian at Haverford College,
Haverford, PA.

Introduction

The term "feminization of poverty" was introduced in 1978 by sociologist Diana Pearce in her article "The Feminization of Poverty: Women, Work and Welfare" (Urban and Social Change Review, 11 (February 1978): 28-35), in which she examined the "economic and social consequences of being female that result in higher rates of poverty." She argued that gender cannot be ignored in formulating socioeconomic policies on poverty and welfare. Feminization of poverty became the term under which a multiplicity of social phenomena is addressed, including female-headed families, child support, gender segregation in the workplace, welfare programs, teenage pregnancy, and the socioeconomic policies of the Reagan Administration.

Since 1959, when the U.S. Census Bureau began regular publication of poverty statistics, women have made up more than 50 percent of the poverty population. By 1980, women comprised 62 percent of poor adults, and attention turned to the one in seven American families headed by women. These families are more than four times as likely to be poor as couple-headed families. "In 1983, 40.2 percent of individuals living in female-headed families were impoverished compared with 9.2 percent of persons in all families." (U.S. Congress. House. Committee on Government Operations, Opportunities for Women in Poverty, Washington, DC: Government Printing Office, 1985, p. 3.) The increase in the number of women in poverty is alarming because "[a]ll other things being equal, if the proportion of the poor who are in female-headed families were to increase at the same rate as it did from 1967 to 1977, they would comprise 100

xiii

percent of the poverty population by the year 2000!" (U.S. National Advisory Council on Economic Opportunity, Critical Choices for the 80's, Twelfth Report, Washington, DC: Government Printing Office, 1980, p. 148.)

While there is disagreement about the causes of the dramatic increase in the number of women and children living in poverty, several factors are widely considered to be important: the decline in marriage rates, and the rise in divorce, separation, and out-of-wedlock birth rates. "The typical outcome of a marital breakup in a family with children is that the man becomes single, while the woman becomes a single parent." (Diana Pearce and Harriette McAdoo, Women and Children: Alone and in Poverty, Washington, DC: National Advisory Council on Economic Opportunity, 1981, p. 9.) Women and children are denied a share of the major breadwinner's earnings; less than half of the women who are awarded child support actually receive it.

Although women are well represented in the labor force, they are clustered in lower-paying, lower-status service jobs. "[I]t is true that more American women are employed now than at any time in this century, but for women, employment is not necessarily an antidote to poverty. The jobs that are available to us are part of the problem." (Barbara Ehrenreich and Karen Stallard, "The Nouveau Poor," Ms. July/August 1982, p. 220.) Women on the average earn only about 60 percent of what men earn. Such factors as segregation in the workplace, lack of job mobility, and lack of flex-time leave women and their children in an economically vulnerable status. Women's income is further reduced by the lack of affordable child care. For many women child care becomes the central issue when deciding whether to work, which hours to work, and where to seek employment.

Another phenomenon which helps to account for the feminization of poverty is the growing number of elderly women. Three-fourths of the elderly poor are women without adequate pensions, health care, or housing.

These women are not experiencing the improved economic status of elderly couples who receive increased social security and pension benefits. Women are treated unfairly by the social security system. Furthermore, women's pension income is often low either because they did not work outside the home or worked in low-paying jobs.

To assist women and children below the poverty level, the federal government funds the primary welfare program, Aid to Families with Dependent Children (AFDC), which was originally enacted as part of the Social Security Act of 1935 to help poor widows and their children. In 1986, over 3.5 million households received average monthly payments of $355 from AFDC. (Statistical Abstract of the United States 1989, Washington, DC: Government Printing Office, 1989, Table 607.) Critics attack AFDC or "welfare" as being at least partly responsible for the increase in poor female-headed households with children, especially in the black community, because it grants aid only to women and children whose husbands and fathers are absent.

The Reagan Administration's Omnibus Reconciliation Act (OBRA) of 1981 resulted in reduced benefits and a loss of eligibility for many recipients working but earning poverty-level wages. Most of those affected were poor women and their children. Many women were also denied Medicaid benefits for themselves and their children as a result of the stricter requirements.

In 1988, Congress, bowing to political pressure for welfare reform, passed the Family Support Act (Public Law 100-485) which strengthened child-support enforcement procedures, required states to implement work, education, and training programs for welfare mothers; required states to pay welfare benefits to poor two-parent families; and offered extended child-care and medical benefits to families in which a parent left the welfare rolls for a job.

The Feminization of Poverty
in the United States

1 Poverty in America: A Definition for Today

"[Poverty] has begun to decline but it is still going up."

Ronald Reagan, 1984, first presidential
television debate with Walter Mondale

During the past 50 years, large social insurance
programs like Social Security, unemployment insurance,
workers' compensation, government employee pensions,
Medicare, and veterans' pensions, as well as the major
welfare programs (Aid to Families with Dependent
Children, Supplemental Security Income, food stamps,
Medicaid, and public housing) have reduced the
percentage of Americans living in poverty. Also, although
the absolute standard of living of the poor has been raised,
they continue to earn less and receive less relative to the
rest of the population.

The War on Poverty began in the Johnson
Administration with the Economic Opportunity Act of
1964, which sought to ameliorate unacceptably low levels
of living endured by a large segment of the population and
to remove the obstacles that prevented upward mobility.
Government policies were directed to fostering high
employment and economic growth, providing education
and training programs for those with inadequate skills and
restructuring the labor market.

Though there is mobility in and out of poverty, the majority of the poor have consistently low earnings despite periods of economic growth, and their progress seems more a result of government assistance than of individual advancement. There is evidence, however, that reducing unemployment does more to reduce poverty than does economic growth. But studies show that because of the cumulative effects of extreme poverty, many disadvantaged people who do earn high school diplomas are graduating to unemployment.

> They suffer from the concentrated effects of poverty. They don't develop habits associated with regular work because their lives are not organized around work. They are crippled in inner-city schools. They don't express themselves as freely. And they are isolated from the job network so important in finding employment.
>
> Professor William Julius Wilson, University of Chicago ("Separate and Unequal: a View From the Bottom," New York Times, 1 March 1988, p. A12, col. 1)

In 1988, the proportion of white Americans living in poverty declined significantly while the proportion of black and Hispanic poor increased, according to the Census Bureau. The growing disparities in income among different groups reflect several demographic trends including the growth of female-headed families, especially in the black community. Most poor people are white not black, though the poverty rate remains three times higher for blacks than whites; 14 percent of the elderly aged 65 or over are poor; 14 percent of the poor live in inner-city ghettos; although the poverty rate of female-headed families is more than four times that of male-headed families, most poor people live in male-headed households; most poor adults aged 22 to 64 are working or looking for work; and only slightly over a third of poor families receive cash welfare benefits. (William P. O'Hare, "Poverty in America: Trends and New Patterns," Population Bulletin 40 (June 1985): 1-43.)

The spectrum of arguments about the causes of poverty ranges from that of Charles Murray in Losing Ground: American Social Policy 1950-1980 (Basic, 1984) to Michael Harrington in The New American Poverty (Holt, Rinehart and Winston, 1984). Murray claims that today's poor are poor by choice. He attributes increasing poverty to government assistance for the poor which rose sharply with the launching of the War on Poverty in the sixties, and claims that public assistance has undermined the black community's work ethic and encouraged the formation of female-headed families which are most likely to be poor. He sees government benefits as large enough to lure many into a life of welfare checks, food stamps and public housing and argues that welfare dependency should be eliminated for the able-bodied non-elderly poor.

Harrington claims that the increase in the numbers of poor people is due to deteriorating economic conditions for younger workers in particular, as well as the loss of well-paid jobs for the lesser-skilled to mechanization, automation, and foreign competition, exacerbated by recession, competition among the baby boom generation, and the rising participation of women in the labor force. According to Harrington, welfare assistance for the working-age poor is still needed, as well as the expansion of government-sponsored job training and educational programs.

1-1. Auletta, Ken. The Underclass. New York: Random House, 1982.

Auletta looks at the underclass in a Manhattan-based non-profit corporation, the Manpower Demonstration Research Corporation (MDRC) which targets the hardest-to-reach long-term welfare recipients, ex-convicts, ex-addicts, and delinquent youths. The program worked best for AFDC (Aid to Families with Dependent Children) mothers who said that money was not the key to breaking the cycle of dependency but rather the fact that others counted on their work and that they were helping people in the supported work program of MDRC. The high placement rate of AFDC mothers resulted from their desire for something better for themselves and their children.

1-2. Beeghley, Leonard. "Illusion and Reality in the Measurement of Poverty." Social Problems 31 (1984): 322-333.

The literature of poverty misunderstands the nature of public assistance. The poverty line is based on the minimum amount of money families need to buy a nutritionally adequate diet, assuming they spend a third of their income for food. The threshold is an absolute measure which liberals find too low because it does not allow for a decent standard of living and which conservatives contend is too high because poor people get in-kind income in the form of public assistance like food stamps and health care. The conservatives believe that by counting all assistance a more accurate measure of the poverty threshold would be achieved.

1-3. Burghardt, Steve, and Michael Fabricant. Working Under the Safety Net: Policy and Practice With the New American Poor. Newbury Park, CA: Sage Publications, 1987.

The authors begin by examining the relationship between the American political and economic landscape of the seventies and eighties and the intensification of poverty. In addition to inflation, unemployment, and the loss of manufacturing jobs, the authors examine the reduction of the social wage, i.e., entitlement benefits and services, in the early eighties. They then look specifically at the homeless, the hungry, older Americans, black single mothers, the disabled, and the new unemployed.

1-4. Couto, Richard. "Appalachia: An American Tomorrow." A report to the Commission on Religion in Appalachia on Trends and Issues in the Appalachian Region. 1984. (ERIC microfiche ED275481)

The extensive poverty in Appalachia is due to the inability of the region to adjust to postindustrial America. The nation's social attitudes and political policies toward the poor, especially women and minorities, make it even more difficult.

1-5. Danziger, Sheldon, and Peter Gottschalk. "The Measurement of Poverty: Implications for Antipoverty Policy." American Behavioral Scientist 26 (1983): 739-756.

Refuting the notion that poverty has declined, the authors find that poverty continues to be a serious problem, although income transfer programs have helped the poor. Census data

indicates that poverty has declined, but the
patterns differ by demographic group. The aged,
female-headed households with children, and the
disabled remain dependent upon income transfer
programs despite the nation's economic growth.

1-6. Danziger, Sheldon H., and Daniel H. Weinberg,
     eds. Fighting Poverty: What Works and
     What Doesn't. Cambridge, MA: Harvard
     University Press, 1986.

     Includes chapters describing welfare
programs, antipoverty policy, household
composition and poverty, and poverty and family
structure.

1-7. Duster, Troy. "Social Implications of the 'New'
     Black Urban Underclass." Black Scholar
     19 (May/June 1988): 2-9.

     Black Americans have been at the base of
the social and economic order. Focusing on black
youth and unemployment, Duster reviews various
issues such as economic structural problems, the
shift of industries overseas or to the Sunbelt, plant
closings, suburbanization, the dual labor market,
and Asian immigration. Black youths who despair
of breaking out of poverty turn to crime and the
rewards of drug trafficking. The private sector is
unable to pick up the slack of high black
unemployment.

1-8. Ehrenreich, Barbara. "Is the Middle Class
     Doomed?" New York Times Magazine,
     September 7, 1986, pp. 44+.

     Since the late seventies, economic
inequality has been on the rise in America, and
some economists predict that the middle class,
which has traditionally represented the majority

of Americans and defined the nation's identity and goals, will disappear altogether. In 1968, the poorest families with children received 7.4 percent of the total income of all families; in 1983, their share decreased to 4.8 percent. This drift began before Reagan and is due to social forces such as divorce which often places the mother and children in poverty but leaves the husband better off. Furthermore, the economy is not generating enough well-paying jobs as it becomes more globalized and service oriented.

1-9. Ehrenreich, Barbara, and Karin Stallard. "The 'Nouveau' Poor." Ms., July/August 1982, pp. 217-224.

The new poor do not fit the stereotypes of long-term welfare recipients and elderly widows. Poverty begins with single parenthood, lack of child support, lack of child care, and inadequate public transportation. Faced with the segregated workforce and lower wages, women are forced to turn to public assistance, which fails to provide even a minimum level of security and decency.

1-10. Gilder, George. Wealth and Poverty. New York: Basic Books, 1981.

The racist component of liberalism asserts that poor blacks cannot make it in America today without vast federal assistance. Liberals insist on income redistribution, an effort to take income from the rich and give it to the poor. Liberal programs diminish the work incentive, cut American productivity, limit job opportunities, and perpetuate poverty. "The only dependable route from poverty is always work, family, and faith." Female heads of families find it

impossible to earn top dollar because of family
responsibilities. Welfare extends and perpetuates
poverty. The best way for poor families to
emerge from poverty is to strengthen the male
role.

1-11. Harrington, Michael. The New American Poverty.
New York: Holt, Rinehart & Winston,
1984.

An anecdotal description of the impact of
international and national trends, such as
deindustrialization, on the poor in America.
Harrington believes that the new poverty is much
more systematic and structured than the poverty
he wrote about in 1962 in The Other America.
He includes a discussion of the feminization of
poverty (pp. 193-202).

1-12. Haveman, Robert H. "Targeting the Poor: New
Policy for the New Poverty." Current 310
(1989): 11-19.

Havemen offers a reappraisal of efforts
by the federal government to eliminate poverty.
The nature of poverty has changed since the War
of Poverty was announced in the sixties. Today,
the poor are mainly single mothers, children, and
youth. Expanding welfare without changing its
structure will not be successful; reform must aim
at equalizing opportunities, not at equalizing
outcomes. Social security retirement benefits,
subsidies for food stamps, public housing, and
student loans, as well as some traditional welfare
programs, would have to be curtailed to allow
targeting of services to youths and the
unemployed, child support, reformed personal
income tax, and savings incentives.

1-13. Hill, Martha S. "The Changing Nature of Poverty." Annals of the American Academy of Political and Social Science 479 (1985): 31-47.

In the eighties, the stereotype of the poor has shifted to the urban poor: unmarried mothers, predominately black, with many children who continue on welfare, along with the underclass of young ex-offenders and ex-addicts. However, an examination of the evidence indicates that the poor are not predominately black, although blacks represent a disproportionate share. Nor are the poor predominately women, although women have become a larger fraction of the poor. Persistent poverty is experienced by only a small portion of the poor. Poverty prevention results from economic growth and government transfers, and an increase in government transfers is essential to prevent poverty among the growing number of elderly and members of female-headed households.

1-14. Kutner, Nancy G., and Michael H. Kutner. "Ethnic and Residence Differences Among Poor Families." Journal of Comparative Family Studies 18 (1987): 463-470.

The authors dispute Oscar Lewis' conclusion that there is a remarkable similarity in the structure of poor families, what Lewis called the culture of poverty. The Kutners investigated six ethnic/residence groups and found the families dissimilar. Black families were predominately female-headed and nonnuclear. Hispanic families were male-headed and nuclear. The authors concluded that there is no consistent pattern of characteristics in poor families.

1-15. Novak, Michael, and Gordon Green. "Poverty
        Down, Inequality Up." Public Interest 83
        (1986): 49-56.

        Though poverty seemed to decline by a
percentage point in 1984, Novak and Green
investigate whether there has been a significant
worsening of equality in income distribution. The
calculation of family incomes has been distorted
by the disruption of the two-parent family,
especially among black families, which accounts
for the severe inequality in income. Two-parent
families are more successful because they rely on
factors of morale, motivation, organization, and
discipline. The shift to single-parent families is a
more important explanation for income inequality
than are policy actions.

1-16. Osmond, Marie Withers, and Mary Dunkin.
        "Measuring Family Poverty." Social
        Science Quarterly 60 (1979): 87-95.

        There is little consensus in the scholarly
literature as to how poverty should be measured.
The standard practice has been to select a low-
income sample from the broader population. This
dismisses relative degrees of poverty and assumes
that the poverty population is homogeneous. The
authors studied black and female-headed families
and found that there were few correlations in
their measures.

1-17. Osmond, Marie Withers, and Charles M. Grigg.
        "Correlates of Poverty: The Interaction of
        Individual and Family Characteristics."
        Social Forces 56 (1978): 1099-1120.

        The authors examine individual
characteristics of family heads and characteristics
of families as they affect job income, employment
history, and public-assistance history. Osmond

and Grigg conclude that the current employment status of the family head is the most important predictor of work or welfare status. The health of family head shows the highest correlation to work history, and occupational status has little effect on the family's welfare history. For female-headed families, being black is associated with more consistent employment but also lengthier dependence on public assistance. In general, the data suggest that families are unable to reduce welfare dependency by improving the work rate of the family head, and families are unable to raise their net income even to poverty level by means of welfare.

1-18. Sawhill, Isabel V. "What about America's Underclass?" Challenge 31 (1988): 27-36.

The persistence and high rate of poverty in the U.S. has not declined over the last 20 years. The poor are concentrated in inner-city areas where crime, teenage pregnancy, and welfare dependency are common. They constitute a growing underclass in American society, one about whom the public is disapproving. The major challenge of the nineties will be to integrate this underclass into the mainstream by strengthening family responsibilities, increasing employment opportunities, and breaking the intergenerational cycle of poverty through education. Recognizing that the persistence of poverty has to do with both individual responsibility and systemic factors, policies must be aimed at weak families, joblessness, and poor education.

1-19. Suitts, Steve. "Patterns of Poverty." Southern
Regional Council, Inc. 1985. (ERIC
microfiche ED 278752)

Although the South has reached new
economic heights, it is also a region of
unparalleled poverty. In 1983, the poverty rate
was approximately 18.2 percent, reversing the
declines of the previous 25 years. Refuting the
notion that public assistance discourages the poor
from working and noting that 79 percent of
benefits go to the elderly and single mothers with
dependent children, Suitts calls for a renewal of
faith, a nation not divided by poverty, and public
policies to stem the rise in the poverty rate.

1-20. Thurow, Lester C. "A Surge in Inequality."
Scientific American 256 (May 1987): 30-
38.

The rich are getting richer and the poor,
poorer; the middle class is having trouble holding
its own. As a result of international competition,
the economy is shifting from well-paying
manufacturing jobs to less well-paying service
jobs, and the shift to low-wage jobs tends to shift
the distribution of income. Reagan's tax and
social welfare policies cannot be blamed for the
growing poverty rates. America is losing out in
the international market and discriminates against
its increasingly female labor force. The solution
will require a higher rate of productivity,
technological overhaul, improved education, and
child-support enforcement.

1-21. U.S. Bureau of the Census. <u>Poverty in the United States</u>. Current Population Reports, Series P-60. Washington, DC: Government Printing Office. Annual. (C 3.186/22)

This report presents social and economic characteristics of Americans living below the poverty level. The first few pages of the report give a brief narrative analysis of general findings and trends. Data is classified by characteristics like age, race, family type, educational attainment, and work experience. Examples of tables included in the 1987 report are "Poverty Status of Persons, by Family Relationship, Race, and Hispanic Origin: 1959-1987" and "Working Mothers - Poverty Status in 1987 of Women with Own Children Under 18, by Work Experience, Age of Children, Type of Family, and Race."

1-22. U.S. Congress. House. Committee on Ways and Means. <u>Background Material on Poverty</u>. 98th Congress, 2nd Session. Washington, DC: Government Printing Office, 1983. (Y 4.W 36:WMCP 98-15)

Report which details the derivation of federal definitions of poverty, demographic characteristics of the poor in 1982, and trends in poverty 1959-1982, including increases in the number of women and children living in poverty and factors affecting poverty, such as divorce and unemployment. It analyzes federal programs designed to reduce poverty and describes proposals for reducing poverty among several categories of the poor: changes in Aid to Families with Dependent Children (AFDC), child-support enforcement, and the earned income tax credit to help families with children, Social Security changes to help the elderly, and long-term assistance and public service employment for the unemployed.

1-23. U.S. Congress. House. Select Committee on Children, Youth, and Families. Domestic Priority: Overcoming Family Poverty in America. 100th Congress, 2nd Session. Washington, DC: Government Printing Office, 1988. (Y 4.C 43/2:P 86/3)

    Hearing held to examine family poverty in America. In 1987, one in two low-income householders worked and of those, one-third worked full-time year round. The Committee invited Daniel Ellwood, William Julius Wilson, Lawrence Mead, and Lisbeth Schorr to describe family poverty in America, its impact on various family groups, and strategies for alleviating poverty. Policy suggestions included improved child-support collection, prevention of teenage pregnancy, and improved job-training programs.

1-24. U.S. Congress. Senate. Committee on Labor and Human Resources. Poverty in the 1980's. 100th Congress, 1st Session. Washington, DC: Government Printing Office, 1988. (Y 4.L 11/4:S. hrg. 100-433)

    Senate hearing composed primarily of the testimony of Michael Harrington and Mary-Jo Bane. Harrington describes the impact of the new economy on poverty. Since 1953, more than 50 percent of America's new jobs have been low-wage jobs. He also discusses the debate on welfare, claiming that most welfare mothers want to work. Bane concentrates on the stereotypes of poverty, pointing out that poverty is not confined to the urban ghetto and that families of the working poor still account for the largest proportion of poor children. Robert Greenstein, Director of the Center on Budget Priorities, concludes that the performance of the economy and retrenchment in social programs have been prime factors in the increase of poverty in the eighties.

1-25.   "The Urban Underclass." Society 21 (1983): 34-86.

This set of articles describes the seriousness of inner-city social problems. Despite a period of unprecedented civil rights activity and antidiscrimination legislation, the position of the urban underclass has deteriorated. William Julius Wilson and others maintain that the problems of the inner city go beyond race or discrimination and increasingly relate to broader issues of societal organization. Class conflict underscores the welfare debate, with liberals refusing to compromise and accept a less than perfect program. Wilson calls for public policies that benefit all the poor, not just poor minorities.

1-26.   Whitman, David, and Jeannye Thornton. "A Nation Apart: The Black Underclass." U.S. News and World Report, March 17, 1986, pp. 18-21.

There has been an alarming emergence of a black American underclass. Separate from the black middle class, the underclass does not share mainstream values. It is composed of an irreducible core of poor inner-city blacks, trapped by joblessness, broken homes, welfare, drugs, and violence. Liberals argue for increased job opportunities and conservatives for bootstrap methods. Under Reagan the national mood has shifted as the public questions outlays for public assistance. The quick transformation of the urban job market has left almost half of the nine million eligible black men out of the job market, making marriage difficult and causing the collapse of ghetto institutions.

1-27. Wilson, William Julius. <u>The Declining Significance of Race</u>. 2nd ed. Chicago: University of Chicago Press, 1980.

"This book is a study of race and class in the American experience." The preoccupation with race and racial conflict obscures fundamental problems that derive from issues of race and class; black and white relations need a broader historical perspective than either racism or class provides. The fairly recent crystallization of the black class structure makes it difficult to speak of a uniform black experience of minority status. Talented and educated blacks are experiencing unprecedented job opportunities, while poorly trained and educationally limited blacks of the inner city see their job prospects increasingly restricted to the low-wage sector. In the economic realm, the black experience has moved from economic racial oppression experienced by virtually all blacks to economic subordination for the black underclass.

1-28. Wilson, William Julius. <u>The Truly Disadvantaged</u>. Chicago: University of Chicago Press, 1987.

Wilson argues that as middle-class blacks have left inner-city neighborhoods, a disproportionate concentration of the disadvantaged has been left behind. Thus, young black children "will seldom interact on a sustained basis with people who are employed or with families that have a steady breadwinner". He emphasizes social isolation, not the culture of poverty. Wilson argues that the sharp rise of black female-headed families is directly related to increasing black male joblessness. He urges that public policy be implemented to improve employment opportunities for both men and women. Furthermore, solutions should not be race-specific.

1-29. Winnick, Andrew J. "The Changing Distribution of Income and Wealth in the United States, 1960-1985: An Examination of Movement Toward Two Societies, Separate and Unequal." In Families and Economic Distress: Coping Strategies and Social Policy, pp. 232-260. Edited by Patricia Voydanoff and Linda C. Majka. Newbury Park, CA: Sage Publications, 1988.

Winnick examines changes in the distribution of income that accelerated during the Reagan years, although they began before that. With the aid of numerous tables, he discusses the shrinking middle class and the fact that the poor are getting poorer and pays special attention to the unequal burden of poverty on racial minorities, children, women, and teenage mothers. He concludes that "the United States is in the midst of a serious polarization in the distribution of income." (p. 257)

1-30. Zinn, Maxine Baca. "Family, Race, and Poverty in the Eighties." Signs 14 (1989): 856-874.

Zinn examines two models of the black underclass, the cultural deficiency model and the structural model. "The argument that the Black community is devastating itself fits neatly with the resurgent conservatism that is manifested among black and white intellectuals and policy makers." (p. 859) Zinn also examines the structural models of poverty that, unlike the popularized cultural-deficiency model, are rooted in theory and research. She argues that while the feminization-of-poverty approach has tended to neglect the way in which race produces different routes to poverty, structural discussions of the underclass pay far too little attention to how gender produces different routes to poverty for black and Hispanic women and men.

2 The Feminization of Poverty

Poverty was seen to be sex neutral in 1940, when more than 90 percent of all families included a husband and wife. But by 1980, 62 percent of poor adults were women, and increasingly poverty has become a women's issue. Two out of three adults in poverty are women. Women heads of households who are raising young children are experiencing a steady decline in their economic status. Changes in family structure, in women's position in the workforce, in the nature of public services for women and children, and in the national economy have all contributed to an increase in both the absolute number of women who are poor and the proportion of the poor who are women.

Diana Pearce, in her article "The Feminization of Poverty: Women, Work and Welfare" (Urban and Social Change Review 24 [February 1978]: 28-36), noted the paradox of women's greater labor-force participation and their increasing pauperization and dependence on welfare. In this article she introduced the concept of the feminization of poverty and argued that the public welfare system along with the sex-segregated workplace tended to institutionalize sexual inequality and oppress all women as well as those already in poverty.

Women's economic status has declined despite the increased numbers of women in the workforce, affirmative action, and the increasing employment of better-educated women. Women continue to lag behind men in their

21

earnings. Pearce argues that an increasing number of women are poor because they are women and that there are economic and social consequences of being female that result in higher rates of poverty. Women are not protected from poverty by either their earned income or public and private transfer income. Women's poverty is perpetuated by the structure of the welfare system, which trades their dependence for insubstantial benefits.

One of the reasons that women are poor is that they continue to carry the major burden of childrearing. The sex-role socialization of women encourages them to make career choices that anticipate childbearing and child care. The second major source of poverty among women is that limited opportunities are available to them in the labor market. Occupational segregation, sex discrimination and sexual harassment together limit both income and mobility for women workers.

2-1. Abramovitz, Mimi. Regulating the Lives of
      Women: Social Welfare Policy from
      Colonial Times to the Present. Boston:
      South End Press, 1988.

Concentrating on the family ethic to
illuminate the relationship between women and
the welfare state, Abramovitz finds that this ethic
has women marrying and having children while
being supported by and subordinate to a male
breadwinner. This ethic underlies welfare policies
and is the basis for distinguishing between
deserving and undeserving women: widows are
deserving, single parents are not. Social Security
programs favor married over single persons,
homemakers over working wives, and one-earner
over two-earner couples. As a socialist feminist,
Abramovitz argues that the family ethic, derived
from patriarchal social thought, articulates and
rationalizes the terms of the gender division of
labor, i.e., the assignment of homemaking and
child-care responsibilities to women. For single
mothers on welfare, the state substituted itself for
the absent male breadwinner to approximate the
normal family.

2-2. The American Woman. Annual. New York:
      Norton, 1987- .

Annual volume prepared by the Women's
Research and Education Institute of the
Congressional Caucus for Women's Issues.
Chapters on women and the family and women
and the economy include discussions of the
feminization of poverty and related issues, such as
divorce, child care, and comparable worth. Each
volume includes a statistical appendix containing
information on family types, income,
employment, unemployment, and poverty.

2-3. Bassi, Laurie J. "Poverty Among Women and Children - What Accounts for the Change." American Economic Review 78 (1988): 91-95.

There is a growing number of women who head poor households, along with skyrocketing poverty among children. This study attempts to untangle the effect of welfare benefits on the poverty rates of women and children. The effect of these benefits varies dramatically by race. The tangle seems to indicate one effective method for decreasing childhood poverty, and that is to increase the earnings of low-income men. This will reduce the poverty among the children they support.

2-4. Cahan, Vicky. "The Feminization of Poverty: More Women are Getting Poorer." Business Week, January 28, 1985, pp. 84-85.

Even as greater numbers of women climb corporate ladders and earn more than ever before, millions are left behind in poverty, particularly women maintaining families. The reasons for growing poverty among women are divorce, widowhood, retirement, teenage pregnancy, low-paying jobs, and lack of health benefits. Women need child-care and medical benefits while they train.

2-5. Corcoran, Mary, Greg J. Duncan, and Martha S. Hill. "The Economic Fortunes of Women and Children: Lessons from the Panel Study of Income Dynamics." Special Issue: Women and Poverty. Signs 10 (1984): 232-248.

Using data from the Panel Study of Income Dynamics (PSID), which has followed the economic fortunes of a nationally representative sample of American families since 1968, the authors dispel some widely held beliefs about poverty, welfare, women's wages, and race differences. They found that two-thirds of the wage gap between white men and white women and three-quarters of the gap between white men and black women cannot be accounted for by sex differences in skills, work participation, or labor-force attachment; changes in family structure over time profoundly affect the economic fortunes of women and children. Arguments about the culture of poverty and the underclass are not consistent with evidence from the PSID about the extent, duration, and nature of poverty; women and children have a much lower and more unstable per capita family income over time and a higher risk of falling into poverty than do white men.

2-6. Cornwell, Gretchen T., and Jenny S. Thorsen. "Rural Women of Pennsylvania: A Demographic Profile." Center for Rural Women, Pennsylvania State University. 1985. (ERIC microfiche ED267939)

While rural Pennsylvania women differ from their urban counterparts in income and education, they fare better as heads of households. Compared to their counterparts in 1960 and 1970, rural women are better educated, more active in the labor force, have higher incomes, marry later, have fewer children, and are more likely to experience divorce and spend most of their later years as widows. They work in traditionally female jobs, and their incomes are lower than men's.

2-7. Ehrenreich, Barbara, and Frances Fox Piven. "The
Feminization of Poverty: When the
'Family-Wage System' Breaks Down."
Dissent 31 (1984): 162-170.

"If the trends of 1967-1978 continue, by
the year 2000, poverty in the US will be almost
entirely concentrated among women and children."
The primary reason for this appears to be that as
the number of female-headed households has
increased, mainly as a result of divorce, the wage-
earning capacity of females has remained at 59
percent of that of males, actually down from 60
percent in the fifties. Social welfare programs
continue to aid many such women, but these are
likely to be cut back; in any case, such programs
as Aid to Families with Dependent Children are
not only demoralizing but insufficient. Solutions
may be found in programs geared to increasing
female participation in the labor force and in
society.

2-8. Folbre, Nancy. "Exploitation Comes Home: A
Critique of the Marxian Theory of Family
Labor." Cambridge Journal of Economics
6 (1982): 317-329.

Age and sex differences have significant
impact on how family members are employed.
Women and children, lacking access to
independent means of livelihood, are likely to
continue to cooperate within a patriarchal family
despite its inequalities. If their economic
prospects outside the family are gloomy, their
bargaining power within the family is quite
limited. As their economic independence
becomes more viable, they may exercise their
enhanced bargaining power to change the pattern
of distribution within the family, rather than
simply deserting the family altogether.

2-9. Folbre, Nancy. "The Pauperization of Motherhood: Patriarchy and Public Policy in the United States." Review of Radical Political Economics 16 (1984): 72-88.

Societal patriarchy fosters inequitable distribution of the costs of raising children between women on the one hand, and men, employers, and taxpayers on the other. The recognition of childrearing as productive labor would entail considerable redistribution of income from wage earners to home workers and from men to women. However, economists look at childbearing and childraising as a luxury in which women indulge. The tax system hurts women's long-run prospects in the labor market by discouraging transitions from family work to marketplace work. Women who receive public transfers by virtue of their relationship to a deceased husband or a paying job are far better off than women who receive transfers because they are indigent mothers. That the welfare system reinforces gender inequality is further evidence of the patriarchal system at work.

2-10. Froines, Ann, and Nancy Hoffman, eds. "Linking the University and the Community: The Conference on Women and Poverty in Massachusetts." Women's Studies Quarterly 13 (1985): 2-5.

Report on a 1984 conference held at the University of Massachusetts (Boston) which pooled the resources of community and university women in order to investigate the problems of women in poverty and to hear first-hand accounts of racism and other forms of discrimination. Participants also planned to build networks among groups who have organized around the social and economic issues raised by poverty.

2-11. Garfinkel, Irwin, and Sara McLanahan. "The
        Feminization of Poverty: Nature, Causes,
        and a Partial Cure." In <u>Poverty and
        Social Welfare in the United States</u>, pp.
        27-52. Edited by Donald Tomaskovic-
        Devey. Boulder, CO: Westview, 1988.

        The authors argue that while the
proportion of female-headed families who are
poor has not increased, economic status of other
families has improved and the number of female-
headed families has increased tremendously.
They attribute poverty among female-headed
families to the lower earnings capacity of women,
the lack of child support, and inadequate public
assistance.

2-12. Gimenez, Martha E. "The Feminization of Poverty:
        Myth or Reality." <u>Insurgent Sociologist</u>
        14 (1987): 5-30.

        From a Marxist-feminist perspective,
Gimenez questions the feminization of poverty
thesis, which does not explain why some women
are poor and others are not. Class analysis
expands the causal analysis of the feminization of
poverty beyond sexism. Today, the majority of the
poor are children under 18 and adults under 44.
In absolute numbers there are more poor women
than poor men, but men experienced a dramatic
rise in poverty during 1978-1983, and since 1983
their condition has improved. It is not age, sex, or
racial/ethnic characteristics that cause people to
fall into poverty, but their social class.

2-13. Kniesner, Thomas J., Marjorie McElroy, and
Steven Wilcox. "Family Structure, Race,
and the Feminization of Poverty." Social
Science 71 (1986): 6-10.

Women's poverty is overwhelmingly due
to female family headship. Divorce and out-of-
wedlock births were the two most common factors
that caused women to become heads of
households. Black women became heads of poor
households four times more often than white
women, and they were more likely to become
heads of households due to out-of-wedlock births.
White women escaped poverty at twice the rate of
black women and benefited more from a stronger
economy. Thirty-seven percent of white women
escaped poverty by marriage or remarriage
compared to 17 percent for black women. Black
women escape poverty by changing their family
structure, e.g., living in their mother's home.
Entry into and exit from poverty is strongly
influenced by marital and childbirth decisions.

2-14. Lefkowitz, Rochelle, and Ann Withorn, eds. For
Crying Out Loud. New York: Pilgrim
Press, 1986.

The editors' aim is to provide a more
complex picture of women's poverty than has
emerged in the media or in the recent literature.
They include essays on the causes of women's
poverty, personal stories of women in poverty, and
possible solutions. Contributors include Diana
Pearce, Barbara Ehrenreich, and Frances Fox
Piven.

2-15. McLanahan, Sara S., Annemette Sorensen, and
Dorothy Watson. "Sex Differences in
Poverty, 1950-1980." Signs 15 (1989): 102-
123.

The authors examine the trend known as
the feminization of poverty, when it began, what it
tells about women's poverty, and what can be
done to reverse it. They examine sources of sex
differences in poverty rates and trends in the
sex/poverty ratio (the ratio of women's poverty
rate to men's poverty rate), which were due
primarily to changes in parental obligations. They
conclude that between 1950 and 1980, women's
poverty rate increased relative to men's across all
age groups and races. The authors advocate
increased income security for two-parent families,
increased earnings and child support for single
parents, and a "greater recognition by the state
that all of its citizens have a vested interest in the
health and well-being of children" (p. 122).

2-16. McLaughlin, Diane K., and Carolyn E. Sachs.
"Poverty in Female-Headed Households:
Residential Differences." Rural Sociology
53 (1985): 287-306.

The majority of poor families are headed
by women, and female-headed families are the
most likely to have incomes below the poverty
level. But there are important differences in
poverty by residence. In 1986, the poverty
incidence for persons outside metropolitan areas
was 18.1 percent and 12.3 percent for those in
metropolitan areas. Non-metropolitan poverty is
explained by poorer employment opportunities,
poorer human capital, and demographic
differences. More traditional family roles for
women in non-metropolitan areas increase the
size of their families and decrease their job skills.
They work fewer hours at less-skilled jobs for less
pay. They receive lower welfare benefits, making

it likely that female-headed households will be poor. Government intervention could alleviate the poverty through education and job training and increased welfare benefits.

2-17. Moran, Kathleen. "Preface to a Feminist Theory of Poverty." Feminist Issues 4 (1984): 59-78.

Sexual inequality creates an ever-expanding underclass of impoverished women and children. Reaganomics mandates that this population bear a disproportionate share of the burden of economic recovery. In reality this is a thinly disguised attack on women of color. The compensatory structures built into a male-dominated economic system reward middle-class women for their silence and coerces women of color into theirs. Feminists seek democratization of work, reprioritization of national budgets away from the "production of death," the reform of the health-care system, the ending of racial and sexual discrimination, the guarantee of full employment, and adequate income supports.

2-18. Nordquist, Joan. The Feminization of Poverty. Contemporary Social Issues: A Bibliographic Series, No. 6. Santa Cruz, CA: Reference and Research Services, 1987.

This unannotated bibliography is divided into three sections presenting background materials, subject materials, and resources. Section one presents a list of citations on the underclass, employment, housing, poverty, etc., back to 1970. The main section on the feminization of poverty consists of five subsections: general, minority women, older women, divorced women, and statistics. Section three concludes with a list of bibliographies and a

list of organizations such as the National
Committee on Pay Equity and the Urban
Institute. This publisher also produces The Left
Index.

2-19. Pearce, Diana. "The Feminization of Poverty:
Women, Work and Welfare." Urban and
Social Change Review 24 (1978): 28-35.

In this ground-breaking article, Pearce
attributes women's poverty to gender factors.
Despite women's increased participation in the
labor force, their earnings have fallen. Women
suffer limited occupational opportunity, are viewed
as temporary/secondary workers, are paid lower
wages, and are forced into longer periods of
unemployment. They receive private transfers of
money in the form of child support and public
transfers such as Aid to Families with Dependent
Children (AFDC), but such income does not
allow escape from poverty. Comparing these
public transfers to those which men receive, e.g.,
social security, unemployment insurance, veterans'
benefits, the public source of money for women
reflects sexual inequality and perpetuates poverty.

2-20. Pearce, Diana, and Harriette McAdoo. "Women
and Children: Alone and in Poverty."
Center for National Policy Review,
Catholic University Law School,
Washington, DC. 1981. (ERIC
microfiche ED229453)

Pearce and McAdoo examine the
increasing number of poor women and children in
the seventies. They believe that women are poor
because they bear disproportionate responsibility
for childrearing and because of their limited
occupational options. The authors urge the
dismantling of the dual welfare system that forces
women to choose between welfare and low-paying

jobs and advocate meaningful job-training
programs.

2-21. Peterson, Janice. "The Feminization of Poverty."
       Journal of Economic Issues 21 (1987):
       329-337.

The feminization of poverty seems to
indicate new trends in the declining economic
status of women. However, Thorstein Veblen
wrote about as early as 1899 about the "barbarian
status of women" in the Theory of the Leisure
Class. Single-parenting, low wages, the bearing
and support of children, and an inadequate
welfare system have continued the trend.
Although the Reagan Administration did not
create the conditions of the feminization of
poverty, it did little to alleviate the problem,
and there was evidence of increased poverty and
suffering with the passage of the 1981 Omnibus
Budget Reconciliation Act (OBRA).

2-22. Pressman, Steven. "The Feminization of Poverty:
       Causes and Remedies." Challenge 31
       (1988): 57-61.

The feminization of poverty has increased
the proportion of young children who have come
to depend on welfare. The underlying causes of
the feminization of poverty include rising divorce
rates, the move by women for greater
independence, and increasing numbers of teenage
mothers. The government's insistence poor
women working will not alleviate their poverty, as
their jobs do not pay a living wage. There is no
reason not to provide family allowances similar to
those provided by many European nations.

2-23. Rodgers, Harrell R., Jr. <u>Poor Women, Poor Families: The Economic Plight of America's Female-Headed Households.</u> Armonk, NY: M. E. Sharpe, 1986.

With extensive use of statistics and graphs, Rodgers describes the dramatic increase in the proportion of the poor who are women and children. He explains why there are more female-headed households and reviews the literature on why such households are poor: high rates of unemployment for both men and women, low wages and income, inadequate child support, and the failure of social policy to adapt to the changing role of women. He argues that "the social welfare programs available to impoverished women and their dependents are deeply flawed." (p.94) He describes features of Western European programs, particularly full employment policies, which help to limit poverty, and concludes with a chapter outlining possible reforms, including child care, the earned income tax credit, job training, and changes in AFDC.

2-24. Russo, Nancy F., and Florence L. Denmark. "Women, Psychology, and Public Policy: Selected Issues." <u>American Psychologist</u> 39 (1984): 1161-1165.

The dramatic changes in women's work and family roles in recent decades have profound implications for employment and family policy, but public policies have been slow to recognize these changes. Policies that reflect the stereotype of the two-parent family have become obsolete, particularly for families who are black or poor, and for women who are disabled. Policies must focus on the problems of child care, care of the dependent elderly and infirm, changes in reproductive technology, and the need for educational equity.

2-25. Sarvasy, Wendy, and Judith Van Allen. "Fighting
the Feminization of Poverty: Socialist-
Feminist Analysis and Strategy." Review
of Radical Political Economics 16 (1984):
89-110.

To the analysis of the feminization of
poverty, socialist feminists add the dynamics of
race and class. They argue that the framework of
the feminization of poverty maintains the
paternalistic family by calling for increased social
services that substitute the state for the male
breadwinner and maintain women in dependency.
The authors argue that it is essential to examine
the dual role of women--domestic-care work and
marketplace work--in order to address the larger
issue of women's descent into poverty.

2-26. Scott, Hilda. Working Your Way to the Bottom:
The Feminization of Poverty. Boston:
Pandora, 1984.

Scott uses the term "feminization of
poverty" to mean the whole complex of forces that
keep women in an economically precarious
position while increasing their economic
responsibilities. She explores the feminization of
poverty in the U.S. and Great Britain and notes
that "the model of development offered Third
World women is the same one that has put us
where we are" (p. 38). She describes women's
unpaid labor in the home as being advantageous
both to men as individuals and to the economy.
In her concluding chapter, "Toward a Political
Economy of Unpaid Work," Scott offers a new
way of thinking about society that stresses female
values and elevates unpaid work to equal status
with paid work.

2-27. Sidel, Ruth. <u>Women and Children Last: The Plight of Poor Women in Affluent America</u>. New York: Viking, 1986.

Sidel contrasts the vast changes in the status of women in the last 20 years with the increasing feminization of poverty. She backs up first-person accounts with statistics, historical background, and information on current policy. Chapters cover the demographics of the poor, women and employment issues, welfare programs, day care, health, and older women. Sidel concludes with an overview of Sweden's family policy and outlines her version of a new U.S. family policy.

2-28. Slesinger, Doris P., and Eleanor Cautley. "Determinants of Poverty among Rural and Urban Women Who Live Alone." <u>Rural Sociology</u> 53 (1988): 307-320.

The number of women living alone and in poverty is increasing. In 1980, of all women 15 years of age and older, 12 percent lived alone. Women earn less than men, may not work full-time and are employed in lower-paying jobs. Many elderly women have to depend on their husbands for economic security. Women in Western society have not traditionally been wage earners but been dependent on men who are in the labor market. Women remove themselves from poverty by marrying or living with an employed person. Women with low levels of education, with disrupted marriages, and those living alone in small towns are likely to be poor. While there are opportunities for training and employment for young women to remove themselves from poverty, the elderly relying only on social security payments are likely to continue to be poor.

2-29. Stallard, Karin, Barbara Ehrenreich, and Holly
    Sklar. Poverty in the American Dream.
    Boston: South End Press, 1983.

    An expanded version of Ehrenreich and
    Stallard's article "The Nouveau Poor" in Ms. (see
    #1-9). Including a great deal of first-hand
    information from women in poverty, the authors
    discuss the causes of the feminization of poverty,
    barriers to full employment for women, and the
    effects of the Reagan budget cuts and so-called
    tax reform. They also include numerous cartoons,
    as well as tables outlining budget cuts in 1981-84.
    The authors dispute the trickle down premise of
    Reaganomics and urge the elimination of racism
    and sexism as parts of a feminist economic
    program.

2-30. Tickamyer, Ann R., and Cecil H. Tickamyer.
    "Gender and Poverty in Central
    Appalachia." Social Science Quarterly 69
    (1988): 874-91.

    Gender has become the newest category
    used to explain the exclusion of certain people
    from the benefits of the mainstream economy.
    This study supports the hypothesis that though
    there are similarities in poor male- and female-
    headed households, there are additional factors
    which explain women's poverty, including the
    gender-specific nature of the labor market in
    Appalachia.

2-31. U. S. Commission on Civil Rights. A Growing
    Crisis: Disadvantaged Women and Their
    Children. Washington, DC: Government
    Printing Office, 1983. (CR 1.10:78)

    Drawing on data from the 1982 Current
    Population Survey, the report examines the
    correlation between marital status and poverty

among women, finding that female-headed families, and especially minorities, are disproportionately poor. Among the reasons for the problem: employment issues such as discrimination, concentration of women in undervalued occupations, lack of training, experience, child care, and inequality of education. The report also describes the influence of health on poverty status and vice versa. Throughout the report, the Commission discusses the effects of the Reagan Administration budget cuts on programs for poor women and their children.

2-32. U.S. Commission on Civil Rights. Women Still in Poverty. Washington, DC: Government Printing Office, 1979. (CR 1.10:60)

The Commission held hearings to examine major institutional forces, such as the welfare system, job-training programs and employment discrimination, and child care availability, as they affect poor women. The examination of the welfare system concentrated on its failures, such as unevenness of grants across the states, rather than on reform proposals. Witnesses who testified about employment issues stressed the low-paying jobs available to women and the need to use federal law to combat discrimination. Even when women are able to find decent-paying jobs, they are often unable to find affordable child care.

2-33. U.S. Congress. House. Select Committee on Children, Youth, and Families. Supporting a Family: Providing the Basics. 98th Congress, 1st Session. Washington, DC: Government Printing Office, 1983. (Y 4.C 43/2:F 21/2)

Hearing held to explore how changes in family structure, the economy, and the labor market affect the earning power of families. Includes testimony by Diana Pearce (pp. 35-55) on the economic inequities faced by women, including earnings differentials, lack of unemployment compensation, and the welfare system. Much of the report consists of tables showing the number and income of various family types for each year from 1970 to 1986.

2-34. U.S. Congress. House. Select Committee on Hunger. Poverty, Hunger, and the Welfare State. 99th Congress, 2nd Session. Washington, DC: Government Printing Office, 1987. (Y 4.H 89:99-23)

Despite the title, most of the testimony focuses on the feminization of poverty, not on hunger. Most of the material consists of statistics on the demographics of poverty and changing family composition, as well as discussion of the influence of welfare on the formation of single-parent families.

2-35. U.S. National Advisory Council on Economic Opportunity. Critical Choices for the 80's. Twelfth Report. Washington, DC: National Advisory Council on Economic Opportunity, 1981.

"All other things being equal, if the proportion of the poor female(-headed) families were to continue to increase as it did from 1967 to 1978, the poverty population would be composed solely of women and their children before the year 2000." (p. 148) The Council disputes the notion that the war on poverty had been won by 1980. They found that the change in the ratio of the poor to the nonpoor came entirely from the expansion of federal spending and not from changes in the economic and social structure. Furthermore, the feminization of poverty became

one of the most compelling social facts of the
decade.

2-36.   Wilson, Julie Boatright.   "Women and Poverty."
         Women and Health 12 (1987): 21-40.

         Because women suffer poverty in
a variety of ways, remedial policy must be equally
diverse. Women are poor because of their
household status, because they are adolescent
parents, or disabled, or elderly. Since the United
States tolerates a seven percent unemployment
rate, there will be continue to be poverty,
although the most important antipoverty strategy
is creating a high-employment economy. Other
policies include raising the minimum wage,
providing more extensive health coverage and
child care, improving education and training,
increasing income support for poor women,
enforcing child support, and extending public
assistance benefits to two-parent families.

2-37.   Women, Children, and Poverty in America. New
         York: Ford Foundation, 1985.

         Report on the Ford Foundation's efforts
to address the problem of poverty in families
headed by women. It begins with statistics on
female-headed families, along with reasons for the
increase in poverty among such families. The
second part of the report describes programs
supported by the Ford Foundation that were
designed to improve assistance to poor women
and children. The Foundation has also supported
programs designed to prevent teenage pregnancy
and to help teenage parents avoid long-term
welfare dependency. Includes statistical tables
and a bibliography.

2-38. "Women Still In Poverty." America, September 15, 1979, pp. 103-104.

Modern technology has not kept its promise to democratize abundance, as poverty continues to exist and is unfairly distributed, affecting particularly women, children, the aged, and minorities. Women suffer disproportionately from three remaining institutional forces: abuses in the welfare system, discrimination in job opportunities and wages, and a lack of child-care facilities.

2-40. Zinsmeister, Karl. "The Poverty Problem of the 80's." Public Opinion (American Enterprise Institute) 8 (1985): 8-12.

Though the social welfare policies of the U.S. have certainly improved our lives, nonetheless, poverty is still with us. The social welfare challenge of the eighties is the so-called feminization of poverty. The author concentrates on child poverty and says government spending cuts are not to blame. He says that families need to be rejuvenated and esteem for children must be raised.

2-41. Zopf, Paul E., Jr. American Women in Poverty. Westport, CT: Greenwood, 1989.

Zopf incorporates a vast amount of statistical data into his examination of the feminization of poverty. The "Summary and Conclusions" (pp. 177-191) provide a succinct statement of the problem of the feminization of poverty, its causes and consequences for women and their children. Includes an extensive bibliography.

3 Female-headed Families

No single factor explains the rise in families headed by women. Increased numbers of out-of-wedlock births, increased divorce rates, and an increased tendency of unmarried mothers to set up their own households all contribute to the trend. Those who are currently living below the official poverty line are overwhelmingly women and children. In 1986, 46 percent of female-headed families were below the poverty level, compared to 7 percent of couple-headed families with children. (Statistical Abstract of the United States 1989, Washington, DC: Government Printing Office, 1989, Table 741.) This does not imply that men are exempt from the problem of poverty and economic insecurity but it points to the need for specific focus on the deteriorating economic position of women.

Up to one-third of the women who receive support from the government under Aid to Families with Dependent Children (AFDC) work, but still they are unable to earn enough to support their families. Single mothers have low earnings because they have less education, are more likely to be unemployed, have less experience, and are more likely to work part time. Since 1981, matters have become worse as government programs designed to provide a safety net for the poor have been cut. One drastic change has been the denial of government support to poor women who work, so that increasing numbers of women have been forced to stop working and rely completely on AFDC funding. The relative poverty of women in America is dramatic, whether they work for a salary, receive Aid to Families with Dependent Children or have retired on Social Security.

Suffering occupational segregation and wage discrimination, formerly married female heads of households receive little if any child support. This is due in part to the low earnings of the fathers. Social norms permit men to cease their support of their children when they leave their children. In <u>Women and Children Last</u> (Viking, 1986), Ruth Sidel points out the plight of the "new poor," women who led comfortable middle-class lives until widowhood or divorce left them poor. Sadly, the saying "only a man stands between many women and poverty" is all too true.

3-1. Arendell, Terry J. "Women and the Economics of
Divorce in the Contemporary United
States." Signs 13 (1987): 121-135.

Census data for 1985 reveals that
although female-headed families constitute only 20
percent of all families, they represent 55 percent
of all poor families. In 1985, approximately one-
half of all families headed by women were poor or
near poor. Fewer than 1 in 19 families with both
parents present and fewer than 1 in 9 with only
fathers were poor. Divorce is a primary
contributor to the impoverishment of female-
headed families. It ends the redistribution of
income from the primary breadwinner to his wife
and children. Women and children suffer further
from wage discrimination, the failure of the courts
to enforce child-support orders, the legal bias
toward men in community property settlements,
and the inadequacy of public assistance.

3-2. Bane, Mary-Jo, and Robert S. Weiss. "Alone
Together: The World of Single-Parent
Families." American Demographics 2
(1980): 10-15.

While children in two-parent households
suffering marital discord are often unhappy, the
same should not be true in single-parent
households after divorce. However, mothers are
preoccupied with the emotional disruptions and
economic loss, and children continue to report a
sense of neglect. The authors recommend a new
system of social insurance to cushion the
economic loss after divorce, including
maintenance allowances collected automatically
from fathers, along with housing assistance, child
care, and employment-training programs.

3-3. Bernstein, Blanche. <u>Saving a Generation</u>. New
     York: Priority Press, 1986.

     The special problems of female-headed
families warrant government intervention. While
a growing economy is essential for reducing
poverty, it is insufficient; "a change in social
behavior is the only thing that will reduce poverty
among female-headed families and their children."
Divorce, desertion, out-of-wedlock births, teenage
pregnancy, and limited education are realities
which must be addressed. The key to success is
early intervention to ensure good nutrition and
health, early childhood education, and rejection of
early sexuality and teenage pregnancy.

3-4. Besharov, Douglas J., and Alison J. Quin. "Not All
     Female Headed Families are Created
     Equal." <u>Public Interest</u> 89 (1987): 48-56.

     The feminization of poverty has not
affected all female-headed families equally.
Families headed by divorced mothers do much
better than families headed by never-married
mothers. Never-married mothers work less,
receive less child support and experience more
severe poverty for greater periods of time. In
order to reduce welfare dependency, social
policies have to treat these different groups of
women differently.

3-5. Bianchi, Suzanne M., and Daphne Spain. <u>American
     Women: Three Decades of Change</u>.
     Bureau of the Census. Washington, DC:
     Government Printing Office, 1983.
     (C 3.261:80-8)

     Drawing on data from decennial censuses
and surveys conducted by the Bureau of the
Census, the authors describe changes in the role
and status of American women between 1950 and

1980. They include statistics and discussion of marriage, divorce, and widowhood; childbearing; household and family living arrangements; education; labor-force participation; earnings; income and poverty status. See #3-32 below for further discussion of the report.

3-6. Bianchi, Suzanne M., and Daphne Spain. <u>American Women in Transition</u>. New York: Russell Sage Foundation, 1986.

Bianchi and Spain analyze the major demographic and social changes for women in the post-World War II period, emphasizing women's transition from the private spheres of home and family to the more public spheres of education and paid employment. The authors include chapters on marriage patterns, childbearing, living arrangements, education, labor-force participation, earnings, and income and poverty. Each chapter includes numerous statistical tables, as well as analysis and discussion.

3-7. Bianchi, Suzanne M., and Judith A. Seltzer. "Life Without a Father: The New American Family Defies the Stereotypes." <u>American Demographics</u> 8 (1986): 42-47.

The authors describe the social and economic characteristics of children living with a single parent and the status of their relationship with the absent parent.

3-8. Booth, Alan, David R. Johnson, and Lynn White. "Women, Outside Employment, and Marital Instability." <u>American Journal of Sociology</u> 90 (1984): 567-583.

The dramatic rise in women's participation in the labor force and in divorce

rates prompted the researchers to test whether
there is a relationship between these factors.
They found a modest correlation between a wife's
employment and marital instability. The wife's
income, marital happiness, and marital problems
have the largest effects on marital stability.

3-9. Bradbury, Katherine, and others. "Public
Assistance, Female Headship, and
Economic Well-Being." Journal of
Marriage and the Family 41 (1979): 519-
535.

The numbers of women receiving welfare
as heads of households with dependent children
increased between 1968 and 1975, although most
of the increase in female-headed households was
accounted for by childless women who are
ineligible for welfare. The authors estimate that
about 26 percent of these households were formed
due to AFDC. Welfare benefits, however, do not
prevent married women's slide into poverty upon
divorce. Their poverty is not due to their inability
to work but to the lack of a husband's income or
that of a wider family. Welfare provides a
cushion against the loss of income associated with
becoming a female head, but it does not make
being a female head of household more lucrative
than being a married woman.

3-10. Cherlin, Andrew J., ed. The Changing American
Family and Public Policy. Washington,
DC: The Urban Institute, 1988.

There has been a steady, upward
movement in divorce rate and age of marriage,
along with falling birth rates. Marriage remains a
central aspect of adult life; nevertheless, there is
an increasing separation of marriage and
childbearing. Contrary to popular belief, the rate
at which unmarried women bear children has

gone down for blacks and has increased modestly
for all whites except teenagers since 1970.
However, the proportion of out-of-wedlock births
has increased. Children are less well off than two
decades ago, with greater economic disparities
between rich and poor children. However the link
between changes in family life and the deleterious
position of children is tenuous. Public policy
should attend to the economic consequences of
divorce for employed mothers, by providing child
support enforcement, child allowances, child care,
flex-time, and parental leave.

3-11. Danziger, Sheldon, and Peter Gottschalk. "Families
with Children Have Fared Worst: Within
Only a Generation, the Trend of Family
Income Has Turned from Growth to
Decline." Challenge 29 (March/April
1986): 40-47.

Within the period 1967-1984, the trend of
family income has turned from growth to decline.
Families with children, 35 percent of all
households in 1984, are the focus of this study.
Female-headed families had lower incomes in
1984 than in 1967. There were large differences
in the mean incomes of white and minority
families and larger differences between female-
and couple-headed households. Public transfer
programs took a greater percentage of all two-
parent families out of poverty in 1984 than in
1967, but aided a smaller percentage of female-
headed families and more white families than
black because of higher earnings of white families.
Recent income growth for all families has been
accompanied by increasing inequality.

3-12. Governor's Commission on the Status of Women, Madison, WI. "Real Women, Real Lives. Marriage, Divorce, Widowhood." 1978. (ERIC microfiche ED161778)

This small book presents the unhappily-ever-after stories of real women who had to cope with an end to their marriages. It reviews Wisconsin laws which support single women in their drive towards independence and self-sufficiency.

3-13. Hannan, Michael T., Nancy Brandon Tuma, and Lyle P. Groeneveld. "Income and Independence Effects on Marital Dissolution: Results from the Seattle and Denver Income-Maintenance Experiments." American Journal of Sociology 84 (1978): 611-633.

The economic independence of women affects the continuation of their marriages because it reduces their dependence. The paradox explored in this article is that slight economic changes have greater effects on marriages than do larger changes. Public assistance programs can influence marital stability depending on whether they are high- or low-support programs.

3-14. Hauserman, Nancy R. "Homemakers and Divorce: Problems of the Invisible Occupation." Family Law Quarterly 17 (1983): 65-88.

There are 43 million American women employed outside the home who earn wages and benefits. There are 40 million working women inside the home who receive no wages and only indirectly benefit from employer-provided fringe benefit systems. The homemaker is involved in the production of goods and services for consumption within the home for which no price is set and whose value is difficult to determine. Recognizing the value of the homemaker's services is essential to encourage equity and to promote a concept of choice of work roles and work places. Without such recognition, homemaking will continue to be treated as the "invisible occupation."

3-15. Johnson, Beverly L. "Single Parent Families." Family Economics Review, Summer/Fall 1980, pp. 22-27.

The seventies have seen a striking change in the structure of American families as the number of single mothers increases. Studies show that growing up in a single-parent family has enduring socioeconomic effects on children, leading to greater delinquency, lower educational achievement, and future marital instability. Single-parenting is no longer a time between the formation of one nuclear family and another. Although the labor-force participation of single mothers varies with the age of their dependent children, most of them work and have less education and less family income than mothers in two-parent families. Nearly half of all black families with children, one-fourth of all Hispanic families, and one-sixth of all white families are maintained by single women.

3-16. Johnson, Beverly L. "Women Who Head Families, 1970-77." Monthly Labor Review 101 (1978): 32-37.

Since 1970, about 60 percent of the female-headed families have been formed by divorce. The income of one-third of these families remains below the poverty level. Such families are more likely to have young children, live in central cities, rent their homes, and live in public housing. Even when supplemented by earnings, welfare payments were not enough to lift these families out of poverty. The incidence of poverty was greater among black and Hispanic families than among white families. This was especially true for families with children.

3-17. Kanaskie, Nancy J., ed. "Poverty in Wisconsin." Applied Population Lab, University of Wisconsin. 1985. (ERIC microfiche ED272333)

Eight papers presented at a 1983 conference are included in this document. In one of them, Ann Nichols-Casebolt discusses the feminization of poverty in Wisconsin. In that state, female-headed households with young children comprise 53 percent of all families with children in poverty. Almost 75 percent of these female heads are employed, but employment is not the way out of poverty because of the lack of quality day care, career training, and job mobility.

3-18. McLanahan, Sara S. "Family-Structure and Dependency: Early Transitions to Female Household Headship." Demography 25 (1988): 1-16.

Investigating whether poverty proceeds from generation to generation, McLanahan finds that female headship does appear to be intergenerational. Female headship correlates to welfare receipt, especially for young mothers. She finds traditional hypotheses inadequate to explain this intergenerational behavior of women in single-parent families.

3-19. Mendes, Helen A. "Single Parent Families: A Typology of Life-Styles." Social Work 24 (1979): 193-200.

There are distinct lifestyles of single-parent families which social workers must recognize: single sole-parent; single-auxiliary parent; and titular parent. One of the most important tasks in social work practice with single-parent families, regardless of their lifestyle, is to help liberate families which are tyrannized by social preference for two-parent families. Social workers should encourage additional support for capable and coping single parents and adoptive or foster parents or titular parents.

3-20. Nelson, Barbara. "Women's Poverty and Women's Citizenship: Some Political Consequences of Economic Marginality." Signs 10 (1984): 209-231.

Poor women who head households are more likely to be detached from the political process than poor men. They relate to the state as dependents, as wives, or as welfare clients. Thus women are the beneficiaries of major social programs as wives or mothers, while men receive unemployment insurance, for example, as workers, not as husbands or fathers. Women's lower benefits and continued poverty limit their citizenship participation and their political power.

3-21. Nielson, Joyce McCarl, and Russell Endo. "Marital Status and Socioeconomic Status: The Case of Female-Headed Families." International Journal of Women's Studies 6 (1983): 130-147.

The most-discussed determinant of the low status of female-headed families is gender, followed by the presence of children. In this study of marital status and economic status over time, it was found that women who remained single had the highest mean income, while those who remained or got separated had the lowest. Women who stayed or got divorced had higher incomes than those who remained or got separated. Sex differences in earnings is the single most important variable in explaining the low-income status of white female family heads.

3-22. "One-Parent Families Singled Out For Trouble." <u>Dollars and Sense</u>, Spring 1983, pp. 12-14.

Demographers predict that one-fourth of white children and two-thirds of black children born in the seventies can expect to spend some part of their childhood living without a father. The growth of single-parent families has accelerated, and the largest group of single mothers are those who have been divorced or separated. The factor that most accurately predicts whether a man will be poor is his occupation; for a woman, it is her marital status. The financial difficulties in female-headed households are due to the high cost of parenting, discrimination in the job market, lack of access to child care, and lack of marketable skills. For most women, the only way out of this trap is remarriage, since those who depart from the traditional family model and remain single are penalized.

3-23. Osmond, Marie Withers, and Patricia Yancey Martin. "Women, Work and Welfare: Comparison of Black and White Female Heads of Households." International Journal of Sociology of the Family 13 (1983): 37-56.

Using data from personal interviews, the authors discuss specific work and welfare behaviors of black and white women who are single heads of households. The greatest burden on the women surveyed is the number of children they have to support, which determines rates of welfare dependency. More young white women are on welfare than black, and black women show a higher employment rate than white.

3-24. Rank, Mark R. "The Formation and Dissolution of Marriages in the Welfare Population." Journal of Marriage and the Family 49 (1987): 15-20.

Marriage plays a limited role as a way off welfare for single women with children, particularly for minority women. It is essential that improvements be made in the structure of the labor market for women (e.g., reducing occupational segregation and wage discrimination). Single mothers also need day care and job training, as well as increased enforcement of child-support payments.

3-25. Reynolds, Suzanne. "The Relationship of Property Division and Alimony: The Division of Property to Address Need." Fordham Law Review 56 (1988): 827-916.

Reynolds explores the relationship between property division and alimony in addressing spousal need at the time of divorce.

Despite state statutes on property division to alleviate post-divorce need, the wife can expect, at best, an equal division of property which, added to her lower earnings and unlikelihood of alimony, will leave her at a severe economic disadvantage. To alleviate this feminization of poverty, Reynolds argues that where there is sufficient property it should be divided in favor of the more needy spouse to eliminate the need for alimony, keeping in mind that the wife's interrupted work experience and employment history will prevent her from earning an income similar to her husband's, and that this often constitutes need.

3-26. Schorr, Alvin L., and Phyllis Moen. "Single Parent and Public Policy." Social Policy 9 (1979): 14-21.

The view of single parenthood as a normal and permanent feature of the social landscape illuminates how marital status affects work as well as economic wellbeing. The better a husband provides, the more stable the marriage. On the other hand, the higher the income earned by the wife, other things being equal, the more likely that a couple will separate. Children do not suffer from single-parenting but from the poverty their families experience as a result of marital disruption. The unfortunate and inaccurate stigma of single-parenting affects public policy. Recognizing single-parenting as a risk not unlike widowhood, why not establish single-parent insurance under Social Security and not make it a welfare issue. Otherwise the weakest (children) and poorest (female heads of households) will suffer the most.

3-27. "Single Parent Family." Special issue. Family
        Relations 35 (1986): 3-224.

The traditional nuclear family is no
longer the normative family. There are different
types of single-parent families, and these families
are more prevalent among blacks than among
whites, though the proportion has increased
among both racial groups. The articles discuss
the high rate of poverty, minority representation,
job mobility and low educational attainment of
female heads, employment, lack of leisure time,
the loss of intergenerational boundaries, the need
for high-quality day care, teenage mothers,
families of prisoners, the physical and emotional
health of children raised in single-parent families,
and finally, resources and networks for these
families.

3-28. Smith, Michael J. "Economic Conditions in Single
        Parent Families" Social Work Research
        Abstracts 16 (Summer 1980): 20-24.

The economic plight of the single-parent
family is due to reliance on only one income.
Though all single-parent families studied saw a
reduction in income, few were able to pursue
income maintenance in the same way. Some
relied on Social Security, others on public
assistance. According to Smith, it does not matter
whether single-parenting is a stage in the family
life cycle or a permanent condition; it is essential
that these families be assisted with employment
and training opportunities.

3-29. Spanier, Graham B., and Paul C. Glick. "Marital
Instability in the United States: Some
Correlates and Recent Changes." Family
Relations 31 (1981): 329-338.

The dramatic increase in divorce in the
seventies correlates to certain social and
demographic phenomena. Since the mid-sixties,
there has been a near doubling of the divorce rate
and of the number of female-headed households.
Children still reside primarily with their mothers.

3-30. Takas, Marianne. "Divorce: Who Gets the Blame
in 'No-Fault'?" Ms., February 1986, pp.
48+.

The legal system contributes to the
impoverishment of women and children after
divorce. For example, settlements splitting
community property are the norm in California.
This allows husbands half and wives and children
the other half. In the matter of custodial rights,
punitive fathers have sought sole custody of
children and have been largely successful. On the
other hand, many fathers turn their backs on their
children and allow them to live in relative poverty.

3-31. U.S. Congress. House. Committee on
Government Operations. Barriers to
Self-Sufficiency for Single Female Heads
of Families. 99th Congress, 1st Session.
Washington, DC: Government Printing
Office, 1985. (Y 4. G74/7: F21)

Beginning with the premise that
"employment is still our best hope for reducing
the numbers of female-headed families on
poverty" (p. 2), the Committee held hearings to
address four issues: the problems with AFDC,
the role of support services such as day care and
transportation, successful state and local

programs, and recommendations for future federal policy. Includes testimony from David Ellwood on women who are dependent on AFDC for long periods of time and from the Department of Health and Human Services on federal programs for women in poverty, as well as testimony from representatives of such organizations as the Urban Institute and the American Public Welfare Association.

3-32. U.S. Congress. Joint Economic Committee. American Women: Three Decades of Change. 98th Congress, 1st Session. Washington, DC: Government Printing Office, 1984. (Y 4.Ec 7:W 84/6)

Examines issues raised by the Census Bureau's American Women: Three Decades of Change (see #3-5 above), which found that one-half of American women worked outside the home in 1980, compared to about one-third 30 years earlier. Women are still concentrated in certain occupations, and there is an income gap between men and women. The proportion of the poverty population living on female-headed families increased substantially between 1950 and 1980, from 15 percent to 25 percent for white families and from 24 percent to 59 percent for black families. Includes statistical tables, as well as testimony on employment issues.

3-33. U.S. Congress. Senate. Committee on Labor and Human Resources. Broken Families. 98th Congress, 1st Session. Washington, DC: Government Printing Office, 1983. (Y 4.L 11/4:S. hrg. 98-195)

This hearing focuses primarily on the social and psychological consequences of divorce but also includes a statement from the director of the Bureau of the Census on the economic consequences of changes in family structure (pp. 199-227).

3-34. Wattenberg, E., and H. Reinhardt. "Female-Headed Families: Trends and Implications." <u>Social Work</u> 24 (1979): 460-467.

The decline of the archetypal two-parent family and the unprecedented rise in female-headed families which represent the single largest subgroup of the poverty population, half of whom depend on public assistance, produce untold stress on women. Traditionally, women have not been socialized to raising children alone or to being single again, and when they separate from their husbands, they show classic symptoms of distress compounded by economic helplessness.

3-35. Weitzman, Lenore J. <u>The Divorce Revolution</u>. New York: Free Press, 1985.

Weitzman conducted a study of no-fault divorce laws adopted by nearly every state between 1970 and 1980 and found that they have a devastating impact on women and children. She includes chapters on the history of divorce law, the movement toward no-fault, notions of marital property, alimony, child custody, child support, and the economic consequences of divorce. She concludes that "for all its attempts at fairness, the current no-fault system of divorce is inflicting a high economic toll on women and children" (p. 401).

4 Children and Poverty

In the United States today, the major changes in family life are the creation and increase of impoverished women and children because of divorce and out-of-wedlock births. Fifty-one percent of the 13.8 million poor children in 1983 lived in female-headed families. Since 1969, the poverty line has been set by estimating the cost of a family-of-four's nutritional needs and multiplying the figure by three to determine a family's minimal income need. The measure has been indexed for inflation to keep pace with the annual change in the Consumer Price Index. (Congressional Budget Office, Reducing Poverty Among Children, Washington DC, 1985.) According to this measure, 22 percent of all children were poor in 1983, and 15.2 percent of the U.S. population fell below the poverty line.

Compared with a white child, a black child was almost 12 times more likely to have a never-married mother, was 2.5 times more likely to have a separated or divorce mother, and was 3.5 times more likely to have a widowed mother. Forty-five percent of poor black children, compared to 15 percent of poor white children, are born into poverty. Average black children can expect to spend more than five years of their childhood in poverty, while for white children the time averages less than 10 months. Much of white poverty is short term and associated with changes in marital status or family earnings; black poverty lasts longer and is less affected by changes in family composition. (U.S. Congressional Research Service, Summary of Poor Children: A Study of Trends and Policy, 1968-1984, Congressional Research Service: Washington DC, 1985).

Additional efforts by the federal government to provide for poor children require the government to restructure the current welfare system and assume full responsibility for providing a minimum income floor for all families with children. Other proposals call for restructuring the federal income tax system and reducing or eliminating the income taxes paid by poor families. Working women with responsibilities for child care lack the fundamental services than would encourage employment and advancement out of poverty through working.

The federal government does offer assistance to people who are poor. The federally financed Food Stamp program, is, however, the only assistance available to all families in or near poverty. Aid to Families with Dependent Children (AFDC) provides cash assistance, but its coverage is uneven and the average benefits vary geographically. AFDC and Medicaid, which finances health-care services, are shared federal and state programs. AFDC and Medicaid provide aid to most children living in single-parent families with incomes less than state-established income eligibility limits, which are generally well below the poverty thresholds. This core of assistance is supplemented by subsidized housing programs and by the Earned Income Tax Credit, which reduces the tax liability or provides cash payments for low-income families with children and low earnings, and by school-based meal programs that subsidize breakfasts and lunches for low-income children.

Social policies to guarantee a minimum standard of living have been outlined recently by Mayor Edward I. Koch who set forth proposals to aid poor children in his 1989 budget for New York City: the provision of prenatal health care, lead poisoning screening and window guards, increased funding for child abuse and neglect caseworkers, expanded foster-care services, and preschool, kindergartens, and day-care facilities. (Help Poor Children, Early," [editorial] <u>New York Times</u>, 22 June 1988, p. A26, col. 1.) The state of Minnesota has become the first state to require employers to offer parental leave to both the mother and the father of a newborn child.

("New Parents in Minnesota Gain 6-Week Work Leaves,"
New York Times, 18 June 1987, p. A20, col. 2.)

4-1. "Children and Poverty." <u>Public Management</u> 69
          (May 1987): 2-5.

          One child in four is born into poverty in
this country today. One in five spends her/his
youth in poverty. One in two black children is
poor. Two of five Hispanic children are poor.
Poverty is due to the dissolution of marriages,
unemployment, discrimination, and catastrophic
illness. Social indicators of poverty include child
and spousal abuse, adolescent pregnancy, female-
headed households, and infant mortality (where
the U.S. outranks Canada, France, Sweden and
Japan). A national commitment is required to
end hunger and deprivation, homelessness,
malnutrition, and inadequate education. Low-
income families need income security, education,
employment, health care, family planning, and
family counseling. These efforts require both
public and private investments.

4-2. Evanson, Elizabeth, and E. Uhr. "The Changing
          Economic Circumstances of Children:
          Families Losing Ground." 1986. (ERIC
          microfiche ED268194)

          From an examination of census data from
1967 and 1984, there emerges a pattern of
increasing numbers of children being raised in
poverty. Single-parent families, especially black
families, have suffered income losses. As the gap
between the rich and the poor has increased,
greater government spending on social programs
has not enabled family incomes to keep pace with
rising prices.

4-3. Fuchs, Victor R. Women's Quest for Economic
        Equality. Cambridge, MA: Harvard
        University Press, 1988.

       Fuchs argues that despite major
antidiscrimination legislation and a quarter-
century of revolutionary social change, women as
a group have not improved their economic well-
being relative to men. He concludes that the
biggest source of women's economic disadvantage
is their greater desire for and concern about
children. He claims that it is the "juvenilization"
rather than the feminization of poverty that should
be of concern to the nation and offers several
child-centered policies, such as parental leave and
child allowances, to help improve women's
economic status.

4-4. Halpern, Robert. "Parent Support and Education
        for Low-income Families: Historical and
        Current Perspectives." Children and
        Youth Services Review 10 (1988):
        283-303.

       Halpern presents an historical review of
efforts at parental support and education for low-
income families to alleviate poverty-related social
problems including child abuse and neglect,
teenage childbearing, and school failure. During
the last 30 years, efforts at reducing poverty can
be characterized as benign neglect. Support and
education programs for parents were aimed at the
middle class. For a brief time in the sixties,
American society accepted the belief that low-
income minority families reflected inequality
rather than produced it, and massive efforts were
focused on creating paths out of poverty.

4-5. Hofferth, Sandra L. "Updating Children's Life
Courses." <u>Journal of Marriage and the
Family</u> 47 (1985): 93-115.

There is considerable nationwide concern
for the prospects of children raised in single-
parent and teenage-parented families, especially as
these families and the percentage of children in
them are on the rise and because they are more
likely to suffer from poverty. There has been a
sharp decline in the proportion of childhood spent
with two parents.

4-6. Kamerman, Sheila B., and Alfred J. Kahn. "The
Possibilities for Child and Family Policy:
A Cross-National Perspective." In
<u>Caring for America's Children</u>, pp. 84-98.
Edited by Frank J. Macchiarola and Alan
Gartner. <u>Proceedings of the Academy of
Political Science</u> 37 (1989).

The authors outline solutions to the
problem of child poverty, with comparisons to
European welfare programs, including family
allowances, housing allowances, child support,
maternity policies, and child care. They begin
with a discussion of child poverty and the history
of child policy in the United States and conclude
that recent welfare reforms have been modest,
though the needs of poor and minority children
have become more visible politically.

4-7. Lerner, Samuel. "Services to the Child in the Single
Parent Family." <u>Journal of Jewish
Communal Service</u> 55 (1979): 369-374.

Lerner advocates continued funding for
programs for the Jewish single-parent
family, including day-care centers,
financial assistance, job training, and
provision of big brothers or big sisters

through various Jewish agencies,
homemaker services, self-help groups, use
of marriage brokers, support groups for
women and children, and foster day care.
Innovation and sensitivity are required in
dealing with these newly deserted
families.

4-8. Marshall, Eleanor, and Anjean Carter. Child
Watch: New York City. Report of the
New York City Monitoring Project. 1983.
(ERIC microfiche ED261129)

A review of federally funded medical
programs for the recipients of welfare in New
York City in 1982 found that the working poor
were hurt the most by the Reagan cuts. The
authors reviewed Medicaid, WIC (Supplemental
Food Program for Women, Infants and Children)
and Title V, Maternal and Child Health Services.

4-9. Ozawa, Martha N. "Income Security: The Case of
Nonwhite Children." Social Work 28
(1983): 347-353.

The conservative Reagan ideology, that
the best government governs least, led to cuts in
social programs affecting blacks and minorities.
White children are better protected as their
parents are more likely to be insured under Social
Security for disability, for example, and because
their parents' work histories reflect better
attachment to the work force. Poor children, who
are disproportionately black and minority, are less
well protected by welfare. Ozawa recommends
two reforms to replace welfare and to better
protect minority children: children's allowances
and tax credits. These measures would deal
directly with children's needs rather than the
inadequacies of parental earnings, resulting in a

weakening of the relationship between color and being on welfare.

4-10. Rodgers, Harrell R., Jr. "Youth and Poverty: An Empirical Test of the Impact of Family Demographics and Race." Youth and Society 16 (1985): 421-437.

Rodgers examines the extent of poverty among youths between 1959 and 1982 and attributes it to the increase in single-parent households and unemployment, as well as funding cuts in public assistance programs. Female-headed families experience high rates of unemployment and earn less in the workforce; their child-support and welfare benefits are often minimal. This family structure forces children into poverty.

4-11. Status of Black Children in 1980. National Black Child Development Institute. 1980. (ERIC microfiche ED196527)

Black children in the eighties, by and large, continue to suffer from a lack of governmental responsiveness to their needs for child care, education, health service and employment. Although poverty and discrimination account for much of the disparity in poverty rates, black children are victims of inadequate, underfunded, and misdirected services. The report argues for preventive services, fully utilizing the strengths of black families.

4-12. U.S. Congress. House. Committee on Ways and
        Means. Children in Poverty. 99th
        Congress, 1st Session. Washington, DC:
        Government Printing Office, 1985.
        (Y 4.W 36:WMCP 99-8)

        Prepared for the Committee by the
Congressional Research Service and the
Congressional Budget Office. Part I, "Poor
Children: A Study of Trends and Policy, 1959-84,"
includes chapters on household composition,
unemployment, and federal transfer payments as
they affect poor children. Part II, "Policy Options
to Reduce Poverty Among Children" discusses
cash transfer programs such as AFDC, in-kind
transfer programs such as food stamps and
housing assistance, and employment-training
policies. Part III, "Costs and Effects of Expanding
AFDC," discusses such issues as a mandated
minimum benefit level and extending benefits to
two-parent families. Includes extensive statistical
tables and graphs.

4-13. U.S. Congress. House. Select Committee on
        Children, Youth, and Families. Children
        and Families in Poverty: The Struggle to
        Survive. 100th Congress, 2nd Session.
        Washington, DC: Government Printing
        Office, 1988. (Y 4.C 43/2:P 86/2)

        In 1986, almost 13 million American
children lived in poverty, nearly 3 million more
than in 1979. A report from the Center on
Budget and Policy Priorities (pp. 44-56) shows
how government benefits lifted a smaller
proportion of families with children out of poverty
in 1988 than they did in 1979, a change that is
attributed to reductions in federal and state
programs, changes in the economy that reduced
the earnings of some families, and changes in the
composition of the poverty population. Also
included are reports on several state and local

programs that aid poor children, as well as
statements from poor children and their parents.

4-14. U.S. Congress. House. Select Committee on
Children, Youth, and Families. <u>Children
and Families: Key Trends in the 1980's</u>.
100th Congress, 2nd Session.
Washington, DC: Government Printing
Office, 1989. (Y 4.C 43/2:C 43/22)

Compilation of findings gathered from
investigations conducted by the Select Committee.
The statistics show trends in economic security,
poverty, child care, housing, education, health, and
families in crisis (e.g., experiencing abuse or
addiction). One finding was that the minimum
wage, in real terms, has declined 33 percent since
1981. In 1988, a full-time minimum wage worker
with two children will earn $2,500 less than the
poverty level.

4-15. U.S. Congress. House. Select Committee on
Children, Youth, and Families.
<u>Opportunities for Success: Cost-Effective
Programs for Children</u>. 99th Congress,
1st Session. Washington, DC:
Government Printing Office, 1985.
(Y 4.C 43/2:Op 5)

"This report demonstrates the proven
success and cost-effectiveness of eight major
children's programs. It provides proof of our
ability to improve the lives of millions of
vulnerable American children, while reducing the
need for later and more costly expenditures" (p.
3). The report covers the following programs:
Special Supplemental Food Program for Women,
Infants, and Children (WIC), prenatal care,
Medicaid, childhood immunization, preschool
education, compensatory education, education for
all handicapped children, and youth employment

and training. The description of each program includes a brief outline of results, benefits, and cost effectiveness, as well as an annotated bibliography of studies of the program.

4-16. U.S. Congress. Senate. Committee on Labor and Human Resources and House Committee on Education and Labor. Educationally and Economically Disadvantaged Children. 100th Congress, 1st Session. Washington, DC: Government Printing Office, 1988. (Y 4.L 11/4:S. hrg. 100-430)

Testimony from a range of experts on ways to break the cycle of poverty for the 40 percent of poor Americans who are children. Policy options include programs to prevent teenage pregnancy, access to prenatal care, pediatric health care, expansion of the Head Start program, and parent education. The witnesses all stressed the importance of early intervention.

4-17. U.S. Congressional Budget Office. Reducing Poverty Among Children. Washington, DC: Congressional Budget Office, 1985. (Y 10.2:P 86)

This study examines patterns of childhood poverty and discusses alternative measures of poverty. It describes current federal programs designed to reduce poverty among children or to alleviate its effects. The bulk of the report includes options for reform of cash-transfer programs, including changes in AFDC and the earned income tax credit, as well as changes in in-kind transfer programs like food stamps and Medicaid. The conclusion is devoted to proposals for improving employability, since "the long-run well-being of children depends heavily on the ability of adults in those families to obtain jobs that pay adequate incomes." (p. 129)

4-18.   Zigler, Edward, and Susan Muenchow. "How to Influence Social Policy Affecting Children and Families." American Psychologist 39 (1984): 415-420.

The increasing numbers of poor children reflect an increase in the number of female-headed households as well as changes in federal policy. Decreased federal spending has cut day care, educational programs for the disadvantaged, and welfare, thereby swelling the ranks of the hungry and homeless. There needs to be a broader coalition advocating the rights of children and families, seeking the assistance of members of Congress on issues affecting children and families.

5 Child Support

The lack of spousal and child-support payments is one of the causes of the deterioration of living standards for women and children after divorce and separation. In The Divorce Revolution (New York: Free Press, 1985), Lenore Weitzman documented that a man's standard of living generally goes up following a divorce, while women's and children's go down.

Critics have pointed out two sets of problems with the child-support process in the United States. First, most states use a costly and time-consuming legal process in which each case is decided individually. Hence, there is great variation in awards, and there is no guaranteed minimum award. Nor are they easy to change. Secondly, there is little enforcement of child-support obligations. Weitzman found that most divorced fathers could pay child-support without seriously jeopardizing their own comfort, but did not pay because there was no penalty for noncompliance (p. 321). Because of lack of staff, difficulties in locating delinquent parents, and inability to enforce collection across state lines, states are unable to collect awards on behalf of women and children.

Wisconsin has developed a Children Support Assurance System, financed partially through AFDC (Aid to Families with Dependent Children) savings, under which all parents living apart from their children are obligated to share their income with those children. The amount of the award is determined by formula and represents a percentage of the parent's income. The state collects the support through payroll withholding and if necessary pays the difference up to a socially assured minimum. The state also compensates mothers for work expenses, so that mothers are not relegated to welfare if they do not receive child support.

In the eighties, it became politically popular to support stricter enforcement of child support, not only to make sure that absent fathers fulfilled their obligations, but also to save the government money on welfare programs. Irwin Garfinkel attributes the prominent place of child support in the welfare reform debate in part to the changing composition of the welfare population, from the "deserving" to the "undeserving" poor. (Irwin Garfinkel, "The Evolution of Child Support Policy," Focus 11 [1988]: 11-16.) In 1984 Congress unanimously passed the Child Support Enforcement Amendments which required each state to locate absent parents and to enforce awards for both AFDC recipients and nonrecipients. States were also required to automatically deduct payments from wages when the parent was one month in arrears.

However, even with the new requirements, more than half of all custodial mothers did not receive the payments due them. ("After Years of Debate, Welfare Reform Clears," 1988 Congressional Quarterly Almanac, Washington, DC: Congressional Quarterly, 1989, p. 350.) The Family Support Act of 1988 established a federal Office of Child Support Enforcement and required each state to establish its own to enforce child support for children dependent on AFDC. The law requires automatic withholding from the absent parent's paycheck for orders being enforced by the state agency. It also requires stricter adherence to state-support award guidelines and requires states to meet federal standards for establishing paternity of children born out of wedlock.

5-1. Amott, Teresa. "Put Responsibility Where It
Belongs: Child Support is No Substitute
for Welfare." Dollars and Sense, October
1987, pp. 17-19.

The claims by feminists, liberals, and
conservatives that enforcing child-support
payments will alleviate poverty have coalesced in
Senator Moynihan's (D-NY) "Family Security Act"
which calls for a Child Support Supplement
Program to replace Aid to Families with
Dependent Children. This bill reflects a punitive
attitude towards the poor and preserves myths
about poverty--in particular, that women and
children are poor because their husbands and
fathers have not provided for them. This act also
promotes a strict patriarchal family arrangement:
father as paycheck, mother as caregiver. Child-
support enforcement is central to the Reagan
assault on the welfare state by insisting that
children are a private responsibility. The act
justifies massive cuts in government spending on
social programs. A progressive antipoverty family
policy would guarantee an adequate income to all
children, regardless of their parents' marital or
economic status.

5-2. Beller, Andrea H., and John W. Graham. "Child
Support Payments: Evidence From
Repeated Cross Sections." American
Economic Review 78 (1988): 81-85.

The absence of child-support payments
contributes significantly to the poverty of female-
headed households. When women receive child-
support payments, their families enjoy lower
poverty rates. Lacking such payments, having low
labor market earnings and little access to quality
child care, many mothers rely on welfare. This
situation is worse for black mothers and never-
married mothers. The decline in child-support
rates between 1979 and 1983 was due to the

compositional changes in the population of
women awarded support. They are younger, less
educated, and more likely to be black. Race, age,
education, voluntary agreements, and years since
divorce/separation affect the amount of support
granted and received.

5-3.   "Congress Sends Reagan Child Support Measure."
       <u>Congressional Quarterly Weekly Report</u>
       42 (1984): 1965-1966.

President Reagan supports legislative
attempts to collect child-support payments
including requiring the withholding of money from
parental paychecks. The bill would extend child
support assistance to all families, not just welfare
families. The bill requires the federal government
to pay 70 percent of the cost of enforcement and
rewards states with good child-support collection
programs.

5-4.   Corbett, Thomas, and others. "Assuring Child
       Support in Wisconsin." <u>Public Interest</u> 44
       (Winter 1986): 33-39.

The Wisconsin Child Support Assurance
Program now being developed insures the
economic well-being of children. All who parent
children will be required to share their income
with their children. Unlike welfare, the child-
support benefit is for children only. It has three
basic features: a simple formula to determine the
amount of the award, collection through payroll
withholding, and an assured benefit. These
reforms are recognized at all levels of government
and uphold the moral principle that parents are
expected to support their children.

5-5. Garfinkel, Irwin. "The Evolution of Child Support
        Policy." Focus 11 (1988): 11-16.

        Garfinkel, one of the architects of
Wisconsin's Child Support Assurance System,
outlines the history of private and public child
support in the U.S., then explains the Wisconsin
system, under which all parents living apart from
their children are obligated to share their income
with the children. The rate is based on a
percentage of the noncustodial parent's gross
income and the obligation is usually collected
through payroll taxes. The state, if necessary,
pays the difference up to a socially assured
minimum benefit. In addition, low-income
custodial parents are compensated for work
expenses, so that a mother need not go on welfare
if she fails to receive child support. Garfinkel
attributes the prominent role of child support in
the current reform debate to the changing
composition of the AFDC population.

5-6. Garfinkel, Irwin. "The Role of Child Support
        Insurance in Antipoverty Policy." Annals
        of the American Academy of Political and
        Social Science 479 (1985): 119-131.

        The current child-support system is a
dismal failure. It consists of two parts: payments
from the noncustodial parent, with rates set by the
courts, and Aid to Families with Dependent
Children (AFDC), the government transfer
system, or "welfare." Although such private and
public transfers cost billions, they reduce the
poverty of female-headed households by a few
percentage points. The author finds some
justification for exempting low-income fathers
from paying child support and for supporting all
children in single-parent families through
nonincome-tested programs, e.g., public education
and children's allowances. Garfinkel is in favor of
a child-support insurance system like one

currently operating in five counties of Wisconsin, based on income withholding supplemented by use of AFDC funds.

5-7. Garfinkel, Irwin, and Elizabeth Uhr. "A New Approach to Child Support." Public Interest no. 75 (Spring 1984): 111-122.

The growing number of children living in single-parent families raises the question of whether it is in the public interest for the government to collect child support from parents who live apart from their children. The authors propose a social child-support system in which all children with an absent parent would be entitled to benefits equal to either the child-support tax paid by that parent or a minimum benefit, whichever is higher. The government would realize considerable savings in welfare payments by compelling absent parents to pay what they owe.

5-8. Haskins, Ron, and others. "How Much Child Support Can Absent Fathers Pay?" Policy Studies Journal 14 (1985): 201-222.

Reviewing income and census data, the authors argue that strict enforcement of child support payments would yield $26.6 billion in 1984, coming mostly from upper-income families. Stricter enforcement of support payments coupled with greater uniformity in setting standards of support, as in Wisconsin and Delaware, would contribute substantially to the income of female-headed households.

5-9. Hunter, Nan D. "Women and Child Support." In
Families, Politics, and Public Policy: A
Feminist Dialogue on Women and the
State, pp. 203-219. Edited by Irene
Diamond. New York: Longman, 1983.

Hunter sees the lack of a uniform system
of child support as a form of social control
because it reinforces women's economic
dependence on men. She notes that many
researchers have found that women and children
experience a sharp drop in living standards after
divorce, while divorced fathers experience a gain.
Women should fight for a new policy that
equalizes the burden of child support between
parents, with state subsidies when necessary.

5-10. Nichols-Casebolt, Ann. "The Economic Impact of
Child Support Reform on the Poverty
Status of Custodial and Noncustodial
Families." Journal of Marriage and the
Family 48 (1986): 875-880.

Rather than focusing on alleviating the
plight of the welfare mother, the author turns to
the absent father. The lack of child-support
awards, inadequate awards, and nonpayment of
awards contribute to the poverty status of
children; 35 percent of those eligible for support
live in poverty. The child support assurance
system, obligating the absent parent to share
income with his children at a rate set by law,
would reduce the burden.

5-11. Oellerich, Donald T., and Irwin Garfinkel. "Distributional Impacts of Existing and Alternative Child Support Systems (Incidence of poverty among children living in families headed by their mothers)." Policy Studies Journal 12 (1983): 119-130.

One out of every five children in the United States is eligible for child-support payments. The authors estimate that one out of every two will become eligible for child support before age 18. The present child support system fails to transfer enough money from the absent parent to the custodial parent to reduce substantially the poverty rate of poor children. Even at peak effectiveness, the present system can do little to alleviate poverty for children. The authors propose a reform which is based on the father's ability to pay and a normative tax on his income, as a means of reducing the numbers of children in poverty.

5-12. Roberts, Paula. "Ameliorating the Feminization of Poverty: Whose Responsibility?" Clearinghouse Review 18 (1984): 883-891.

The author is with the Center for Law and Social Policy. She argues that the discussion of the feminization of poverty focuses on the female-headed household which must be allowed to combine paid employment, child support and alimony with public benefits to escape poverty. The issue of child-support enforcement has seldom been explored because of potential conflicts among poor people. In 1984, Congress added Title IV, Part D to the Social Security Act to enable services to both welfare and nonwelfare mothers in establishing paternity and securing child support. This law has potential for improving the child-support collection system.

5-13. Robins, Philip K. "Child Support, Welfare
            Dependency, and Poverty." <u>American
            Economic Review</u> 76 (1986): 768-788.

            An empirical analysis of 1982 census data
attests to the effect of child-support enforcement
policies on poverty and welfare dependency
among female-headed families. Female-headed
households have the highest rates of poverty in
the United States, and the increasing rate of
illegitimacy and divorce will continue the growth
of this group. Where there is a strong child-
support enforcement program in place, it is less
likely that the mother will apply for welfare, but
this does not affect poverty rates. Robins
concludes that child-support enforcement
programs may allow for reductions in welfare
costs, but the current legal system establishes such
low awards as to make child support ineffective as
an antipoverty device.

5-14. Robins, Philip K., and Katherine P. Dickinson.
            "Receipt of Child Support By Single-
            Parent Families." <u>Social Service Review</u>
            58 (1984): 622-641.

            There is interest in enforcing greater
formal child-support obligations of the absent
parent as a means of reducing welfare dependency
in the U.S. For such a program to be successful,
the absent father needs to have a stable income
and to enjoy more liberal custodial arrangements
with his children. The authors view this emphasis
on the noncustodial parent to be as important as
current efforts to increase employment of welfare
mothers.

5-15. Simpson, Peggy. "Making Sure Dad Pays Up."
       <u>Ms.</u>, May 1988, pp. 65-67.

       A bill sponsored by Representative Marge
Roukema (R-NJ) would provide for automatic
deductions of child-support payments from the
wages of all absentee parents, not just those who
are delinquent in payments. The deductions
would be ordered as part of any divorce
settlement or whenever paternity has been proven
in cases of unwed parents. Many states are now
awaiting federal funds to develop computerized
systems to allow automatic deductions. Over the
past decade, child support has come to be seen
not as a social welfare problem but as a legal and
moral one.

5-16. Snyder, Lillian M. "The Deserting, Nonsupporting
       Father: Scapegoat of Family Nonpolicy."
       <u>Family Coordinator</u> 28 (1979): 594-599.

       Deserting fathers are scapegoated by
society and declared offenders by the criminal
justice system. Snyder urges the establishment of
family crisis centers, job training for male family
heads, income supplements for young families,
and the reorganization of health and public
welfare services.

5-17. Stuart, Archibald. "Rescuing Children: Reforms in
       the Child Support Payment System."
       <u>Social Services Review</u> 60 (1986): 201-
       217.

       The increasing feminization of poverty
has impoverished children, as well, and focused
attention on the inadequacies of the current child-
support system. Federal and state legislators have
responded by establishing state agencies to
monitor child-support payment and to authorize
automatic income withholding of support

payments from earnings. A federal system of withholding would simplify collection across state lines and could be tied to the federal tax system. Lastly, a federal supplement, replacing AFDC, should be available when payments fall below a minimum standard.

5-18. U.S. Bureau of the Census. Child Support and Alimony. Current Population Reports, Series P-23. Washington, DC: Government Printing Office. Irregular. (C 3.186/4)

This report presents information on both the award and actual receipt of child support and alimony. The first few pages include a narrative description of findings for the year, as well as trends. The bulk of the report consists of tables which present cross-tabulated results by many variables. Examples of tables in the 1985 supplemental report include "Award and Recipiency Status of Women - Child Support Payments for All Women and Women Below the Poverty Level" and "Receipt of Child Support Payments in 1985 by Selected Characteristics of All Women and Women With Incomes Below the Poverty Level."

5-19. U.S. Congress. House. Committee on Ways and Means. Child Support Enforcement Program. 100th Congress, 2nd Session. Washington, DC: Government Printing Office, 1988. (Y 4.W 36:100-56)

Hearings held to consider changes in child-support enforcement programs. Issues covered include procedures for establishing paternity, alternative methods for determining levels of support payments, and the difficulties in collecting support across state lines. Irving Garfinkel describes Wisconsin's Child Support

Assurance System through which children are
entitled to benefits paid by the noncustodial
parent or to a socially assured minimum benefit,
paid by the state and financed partly through
AFDC savings.

6 Child Care

More than half of all American women with children under six now work outside the home. Only 10 percent of the nation's private employers provide workers with child-care services or benefits. ("Child-Care Bill Dies Amid Partisan Sniping," 1988 Congressional Quarterly Almanac, Washington, DC: Congressional Quarterly, 1989, p. 365.) Working parents find it difficult to locate good quality, affordable child care. Many are driven to compromise and leave their children in unlicensed and less than satisfactory situations. Even middle-income, two-earner families find the cost of quality child care prohibitive.

Child-care costs can be prohibitive for working mothers; a woman working full time at minimum wage would might spend up to 40 percent of her paycheck for child care. Without access to affordable day care, mothers of young children are unable to work or to improve their skills or education. In Child Care: A Workforce Issue (U.S. Department of Labor, Washington, DC: Government Printing Office, 1988), the Secretary's Task Force noted that some low-income families may be torn between choosing whether to work or to participate in training, or to take care of their children, considering the expense of day care. The lack of safe, affordable child care jeopardizes the safety of all children, the integrity of working families, and the productivity of the workforce. Without the assurance that children are well cared for, parents cannot logistically and psychologically work full time.

Currently, the federal government subsidizes child care for poor families through Title XX of the Social

Security Act and through programs such as Head Start. The child-care tax credit, on the other hand, primarily benefits middle- and upper-income families, since many lower-income families pay no federal income tax. The Family Support Act of 1988, designed in part to ease the transition from welfare to work, provides for the payment of care expenses if necessary for an individual's employment or education or training. "Furthermore, child care must be provided during a transitional period up to a year, if it is necessary, when employment enables an individual to leave the welfare rolls." ("The Family Support Act of 1988," Challenge 4 (Winter 1988-89): 17.)

Conservatives favor giving business a tax deduction equal to half the cost of setting up a voluntary leave program, and they oppose proposals to subsidize day-care centers and set minimum standards of quality. President Bush continues the "pro-family" response of former President Reagan and favors providing low-income families with a tax credit for child-care needs. (Steven V. Roberts, "Congress Child Care Bills Pour In and Obstacles Arise," New York Times, 14 February 1989, p. A20, col. 1.) In 1989, Congress was considering rival child-care bills, and it is likely that a child-care act will emerge from the 101st Congress.

6-1. Floge, Lillian. "The Dynamics of Child Care Use and Some Implications for Women's Employment." Journal of Marriage and the Family 47 (1985): 143-154.

Employed women make repeated changes in child-care arrangements, relying on relatives and to a lesser extent day-care centers. Women's choices are determined by availability of services, as in group-care arrangements for children under the age of three. A woman who can depend on different arrangements for child care is less likely to lose her job when, for example, her child is sick and cannot attend day care. On the other hand, many studies reveal that more women would be looking for work if suitable child-care arrangements could be found.

6-2. Hofferth, Sandra L. "Day Care in the Next Decade: 1980-1990." Journal of Marriage and the Family 41 (1979): 649-658.

With greater numbers of mothers of preschool children in the work force and the increasing numbers of preschool children, there will be a greater demand for day-care services. However, since the costs of providing such services are likely to increase, there will be fewer providers of day-care services. The growing incidence of single-parent families will add to this demand and extend the problem of inadequate day-care services to families with infants and toddlers.

6-3. Hofferth, Sandra L., and Deborah A. Phillips. "Child Care in the United States, 1970-1995." Journal of Marriage and the Family 49 (1987): 559-571.

The high cost of child care affects the choices women make about child-bearing and employment. The burden for the provision of child care is too great to remain with the private sector; government help is required.

6-4. Nakamura, Charles Y., and others. "Interdependence of Child Care Resources and the Progress of Women in Society." <u>Psychology of Women Quarterly</u> 6 (1981): 12-25.

The interdependence between the need for child care and the roles of women in society is further influenced by economic conditions and women's aspirations. The provision of child care could enhance women's aspirations. While child care continues to be mainly the responsibility of women, members of many types of families need child care as they seek additional employment or education.

6-5. Rubin, Karen. "Whose Job is Child Care?" <u>Ms.</u>, March 1987, pp. 31-36+.

Since unprecedented numbers of employed women are having babies, corporate America is suffering a female brain drain. A significant number of companies, even those having benefits and policies supportive of employed women, do not offer their female workers either job protection or income protection at the time of childbirth or adoption. While homework, flex-time, and part-time work can be excellent solutions, employers often take advantage of workers taking leave in order to save on benefits. Merck and Company has an on-site day-care program, owned and operated by employees, which management says allows Merck to attract and retain skilled people, as employees do not leave their home problems at home and their work problems at work.

6-6. U.S. Congress. House. Committee on Education and Labor. <u>Hearing on H.R. 3660, the Act for Better Child Care Service</u>. 100th Congress, 2nd Session. Washington, DC: Government Printing Office, 1988. (Y 4.Ed 8/1:100-74)

House hearings on the Act for Better Child Care Service (ABC). In 1985, nearly half of all children under six had mothers who worked outside the home. Witnesses point out that affordable day care is essential to help families become self-sufficient, and that the bill would provide funds to pay child-care workers, most of them women, decent wages.

6-7. U.S. Congress. House. Committee on Ways and Means. <u>Child Care Needs of Low-Income Families</u>. 100th Congress, 2nd Session. Washington, DC: Government Printing Office, 1989. (Y 4. W 36: 100-73).

House hearing held to consider how to best meet the child-care needs of working families, especially those who are poor. The document includes testimony and written statements discussing the consequences of the lack of affordable child care and the ways in which the federal government should act, not only through subsidies and tax breaks, but also through training programs and salary and safety standards.

6-8. U.S. Congress. Senate. Committee on Labor and Human Resources. <u>Act for Better Child Care Services of 1988</u>. 100th Congress, 2nd Session. Washington, DC: Government Printing Office, 1988. (Y 4.L 11/4:S. hrg. 100-882)

Senate hearings held to consider passage of the Act for Better Child Care Services (ABC) bill, which aims to reduce the cost of day care, raise the pay of day-care workers, improve quality, and expand supply. ABC would create agencies in the Department of Health and Human Services to allocate money among the states and enforce new federal regulations. The hearing includes testimony on the limited availability and high cost of day care, especially for women who work at low-paying jobs or who are forced to remain on welfare because affordable day care is not available.

6-9. U.S. Department of Labor. <u>Child Care: A Workplace Issue</u>. Washington, DC: U.S. Department of Labor, 1988. (L 1.2:C 43/5)

The Secretary's Task Force reports on federal and state funding for child care, describes employer-assisted child-care programs, examines workforce trends and the need for child care, and analyzes issues of availability, affordability, and quality. The report concludes that while there does not appear to be a general shortage of day care, certain types of care may be in short supply in some communities. Moreover, affordable child care may be a critical problem for families with incomes of less than $15,000 a year, who may be forced to choose between working and staying home to care for their children.

7 Women's Employment Issues

The percentage of women who are employed outside the home has increased steadily since the beginning of the century, an increase that shows no sign of slowing. In 1987, nearly 60 percent of women over 16 worked outside the home. (Statistical Abstract of the United States 1989, Washington, DC: Government Printing Office, 1989, Table 621.) Nonetheless, the average wage differential between men and women gives women approximately 35 percent less money than men despite their educational attainment, and this ratio has changed little in the last 30 years. Recently, the New York Times (February 9, 1989, p. C11, col.3) reported on a Rand Corporation study of the wage gap between men and women which found that working women earn only 65 percent of men's wages and, although the wage gap is narrowing, an increasing percentage of the poor are women. By the year 2000, they estimate, women will make 74 percent of men's earnings.

As more and more women engage in paid labor outside the home, the segregation of women into a pink ghetto has intensified. The structure of the job market is such that if women in the labor force had no sex-related disadvantages at work, many families living in poverty would not be poor. Half of all full-time female workers are unable to support two children without additional income (the comparable figure for men is 20 percent). Fully one-quarter of poor women who head households work.

In 1987, families maintained by women had median incomes of $14,620, compared to $24,804 for families maintained by men with no wife present. (Statistical Abstract of the United States 1989, Washington, DC: Government Printing Office, 1989, Table 723.)   Nearly two out of three (64 percent) of all minimum wage earners in the United States are women. The new jobs being created in the service sector, filled mostly by women, offer little chance for them to work their way out of poverty. Furthermore, many of the new jobs are in suburban areas, out of reach of poor inner-city women.

Poverty is assumed to be the result of joblessness. However, merely having a job does not guarantee a way out of poverty. Due to inflation, working women earning minimum wage have 30 percent less real purchasing power today than they did in 1981, when the minimum wage was last raised. Although Congress originally targeted the minimum wage to equal 50 percent of the average hourly wage, in 1986 the minimum wage reached an all-time low of 38.3 percent.

Women's responsibilities for nonpaid care-work in their families not only interrupts their paid work time but also reduces their seniority, threatening both their job rights and credit for work experience. This home-work shortens women's paid work careers and lowers their earnings. Furthermore, lack of affordable child care prevents many women from working or from obtaining training that would help them qualify for better-paying jobs.

Despite the fact that equal pay for equal work is the law of the land, women's pay for equivalent work tends to be lower. Jobs which are traditionally women's jobs (such as retail sales, services and clerical jobs) pay less than men's jobs with equivalent skill and training requirements. A high percentage of these jobs are not unionized. For further discussion of the issues of comparable worth and pay equity, see Chapter 8.

7-1. Acker, Joan. "Class, Gender, and the Relations of Distribution." Signs 13 (1988): 473-497.

Marxist analysis of the oppression of women leaves unresolved issues. More satisfying is an analysis which combines gender distribution and gendered relations of production, as distribution is the growing crisis in postindustrial capitalist societies. This is evidenced by the growing number of women and children in poverty, the elimination of high-paying male working-class jobs, and the introduction of new, low-paying, female jobs, particularly in the service sector.

7-2. Axinn, June, and Mark J. Stern. "Women and the Postindustrial Welfare State." Social Work 32 (1987): 282-286.

The hallmark of the postindustrial state is the decline of goods production and the growth of service industries. This has had particular impact on women, whose participation in the white-collar occupations is growing. Women in the service sector are confined to lower-paying, less-secure employment. The new postindustrial economy must extend social welfare benefits to both female and male workers, regardless of marital status, and protect against periods of part-time employment, substandard wages, and long-term unemployment by extending unemployment benefits, job training, and tax reforms.

7-3. Barrett, Nancy S. "Obstacles to Economic Parity for Women." American Economic Review 72 (1982): 160-165.

Despite an unprecedented increase in women's participation in the labor force, women have failed to achieve significant wage gains relative to men and to move out of traditional occupational ghettos. The source of women's failure to achieve economic parity in labor markets is related to their disproportionate commitment to unpaid work within the family unit. Women's household responsibilities compete for time and energy with labor force activities; while for men, household responsibilities (i.e., financial support) are complementary to labor force activities. Gender-based family roles support occupational stereotyping and low wages and defy all remedies.

7-4. Barrett, Nancy S. "Women as Workers." 1984. (ERIC microfiche ED246209)

Women's changing status as they become heads of households and move into the labor market in increasing numbers has led to dramatic changes in attitudes and in law. However, women continue to be paid less than men, resulting in the feminization of poverty. Families headed by women need support services, flexible schedules and part-time work, equity in tax laws and Social Security benefits, day care, and equal employment opportunity.

7-5. Barton, Amy E. "Campesinas: Women Farmworkers in the California Agricultural Labor Force." Report of a Study Project by the California Commission on the Status of Women. 1978. (ERIC microfiche ED167322)

Barton's study of female Mexican-American farm workers in California showed that their annual income was under $3000 and one-third were heads-of-households. They had between one and seven years of schooling. Their incomes were two-thirds that of men. Their employers felt the women were not capable of more skilled or more physically demanding work and paid them accordingly, although the women claimed to be capable of better-paying work.

7-6. Barton, Margaret, George Farkas, and Kathy Kushner. "White, Black, and Hispanic Female Youths in Central City Labor Markets." Sociological Quarterly 29 (1988): 605-621.

Reviewing 1980 census data and comparing female and male and white and minority youths, the authors concluded that inner-city black females continue to be disadvantaged. Their employment and wage rate are lower than that of their male counterparts. Wage rates for young white females are affected positively by education and negatively by responsibilities as heads of households, as well as the local unemployment rate. These factors do not affect the wage rates for black and Hispanic females. Their employers treat them interchangeably and pay them the minimum wage.

7-7. Beck, E. M., Patrick M. Horan, and Charles M. Tolbert. "Industrial Segmentation and Labor-Market Discrimination." Social Problems 28 (1980): 113-130.

Market discrimination against women and minorities is a social and economic reality. It is not simply an imperfection in the marketplace but an ingrained structural feature of industrial capitalism. Using the simplistic but convenient dual economy theory (primary equals higher-paying, secondary equals lower-paying, where women and minorities are concentrated), the authors explore the structural elements of discrimination. Women and minorities do not enjoy the same return on their knowledge and training as do white men, who are in the core sector rather than the peripheral sectors of the economy. This segmentation of the labor market is a substantial factor affecting wage discrimination. Clearly, structural factors at work in the economy are causing the discrimination.

7-8. Blumrosen, Ruth G. "Wage Discrimination, Job Segregation and Woman Workers." Women's Rights Law Reporter 6 (1979-80): 19-57.

One of the primary indications of employment discrimination is the earnings gap between female and male workers, despite Congressional initiatives such as the Equal Pay Act of 1963 and Title VII of the Civil Rights Act of 1964. The history of the implementation of Title VII separates job segregation from wage discrimination, but Blumrosen argues that they are two inseparable issues, that the forces which segregate women's work also lower their wage rates for those jobs. Job segregation does encompass wage discrimination, and, where possible, salaries should be raised in segregated jobs.

7-9. Bokemeier, Janet L., and Ann R. Tickamyer. "Labor Force Experiences of Nonmetropolitan Women." Rural Sociology 50 (1985): 51-73.

Like their metropolitan counterparts, nonmetropolitan women's participation in the labor market has steadily increased. In 1979, 48.2 percent of nonmetropolitan women were in the labor force. In Kentucky nonmetropolitan workers tend to be concentrated in peripheral industries, tend to be in operative and service jobs, and are less likely to be in white-collar jobs. They also report higher unemployment than metropolitan women. Most women's employment is limited to secondary sector jobs which are low-paying, unstable, and sex-segregated. Within the limited opportunities available, increased education leads to better jobs.

7-10. Bridges, William P., and Richard A. Berk. "Sex, Earnings and Nature of Work: Job Level Analysis of Male-Female Income Differences." Social Science Quarterly 58 (1978): 553-565.

There is substantial agreement that wide disparities exist between the incomes of working women and men, and the authors offer a tri-level explanation: specification of sex in employee qualifications, differences by sex in job characteristics, and differences by sex in the way these variables are translated into obtained income. Extrapolating from data on white-collar employees and their supervisors (a survey conducted in metropolitan Chicago), the authors find that female and male white-collar workers are highly segregated by task and occupational level. Among job groups, income disparities in male and female-typed jobs are almost as big as income differences between women and men. These differences cannot be explained by different levels of productivity but reflect prior discrimination and women's different pattern of attachment to companies.

7-11. Brown, Gary D. "Discrimination and Pay Disparities Between White Men and Women." Monthly Labor Review 101 (March 1978): 17-22.

Rather than look at discrimination between the races or between the genders, Brown's analysis explores how white men, usually the employees' dominant group, discriminate against other groups, especially white women. White men get a higher return on their employment: choice of occupation, wage rate, and degree of power. Remediation must go beyond guarantees of equal pay for equal work and must include equal opportunity in obtaining jobs and career advancement, access to credit, and day care.

7-12. Chafetz, Janet Saltzman. "The Gender Division of Labor and the Reproduction of Female Disadvantage." Journal of Family Issues 9 (1988): 108-131.

Gender stratification in the labor market is maintained and reproduced because women are responsible for childrearing and domestic tasks. These differing responsibilities produce power inequities between the genders and are reinforced in the marketplace by men, who are more powerful. Men occupy elite positions in major societal institutions and control the job access and wages of women. A woman's double day (labor market and domestic responsibilities) further reduces her abilities to compete with men for more powerful and prestigious jobs.

7-13. Cooney, Rosemary Santana. "A Comparative Study of Work Opportunities for Women." Industrial Relations 17 (1978): 64-74.

Asking whether women's increased participation in the labor force has lessened sex segregation in the workforce, Cooney found that in nonagricultural employment it did. Integrating women into the workforce has proceeded more rapidly, however, than reducing sex segregation or improving the status of female work. The author urges greater social equality in the labor force.

7-14. Cotton, Jeremiah. "Discrimination and Favoritism in the U.S. Labor Market: The Cost to a Wage Earner of Being Female and Black and the Benefit of Being Male and White." <u>American Journal of Economics and Sociology</u> 47 (1988): 15-28.

When their skills are fairly comparable, black women earn 21 percent less than white males; white women earn 15.5 percent less. This is true despite the fact that black women have more continuous work histories than white women and higher educational rates than black men who earn more. The results of the study on wage discrimination reported here suggest that sexual discrimination may be more problematic for black women than race discrimination.

7-15. Coverdill, James E. "The Dual Economy and Sex-Differences in Earnings." <u>Social Forces</u> 66 (1988): 970-993.

The analysis allowed by the dual-economy theory is insufficient to explain the sex differences in wage earnings. This theory allocates women to peripheral secondary jobs and men to jobs in core industries. Even when work experience, education, and several familial variables are included, women are likely to be excluded from core-sector jobs. The theory masks the many ways that sex segregation works in different economic sectors and conceals the role of the organizations in which women and men work in shaping patterns of sex inequality.

7-16. Donovan, Rebecca, and others. "Unemployment Among Low-Income Women: An Exploratory Study." Social Work 32 (1987): 301-305.

Despite the higher unemployment rates of women since 1948, loss of jobs by women has received little attention in the literature and media. Loss of jobs in the textile and apparel industries have been just as severe as the well-publicized closings of automobile and steel industries. Textile and apparel workers are primarily working-class women, including minorities, undocumented workers, and immigrants. Job loss among unionized women garment center workers in New York City often led to poverty if the women were heads of households, since their earnings (62 percent of men's earnings) alone will not support a family above the poverty line.

7-17. England, Paula. "The Sex Gap in Work and Wages." Society 22 (July/August 1985): 68-74.

This article presents an interdisciplinary analysis of sex-segregated jobs and wage discrimination. Discrimination in hiring, placement, and promotion affect job segregation. Wage discrimination operates at entry-level jobs in which females and males have no job experience and the gender of the job's typical incumbent is taken into account when setting wage levels. It is not crowding in female occupations which causes the low wages in female-dominated jobs but pay discrimination. The pay gap is due to sex-role socialization, less job experience, and discrimination in female-dominated jobs.

7-18. Felmlee, Diane H. "A Dynamic Analysis of
Women's Employment Exits."
Demography 21 (1984): 171-184.

Felmlee explores the issue of the
interdependence of women's employment and
fertility. Studies indicate that childbearing will
limit a woman's labor force participation and that
a woman's labor force participation is a good
predictor of her fertility. In her study, Felmlee
finds several discrepancies having to do with a
woman's education, her husband's income, and
how long she has had her present job.

7-19. Fineshriber, P. H. "Jobless Insurance Inequities
Deepen as More Women Enter the
Labor Force." Monthly Labor Review
102 (April 1979): 44-45.

What will be the impact on
unemployment compensation of the increased
labor-force participation of women and of the
nearly equal proportions of women and men in
the labor force? Women work for the same
reasons as men, as a matter of economic
necessity, and are entitled to compensation for
wages lost during unemployment. Compensation
should be provided for women as unemployed
homemakers upon the death of their husbands.

7-20. Graham, Mary. "Good Jobs at Bad Wages." New
Republic, November 21, 1988, pp. 27-29.

Travelling two hours on three buses from
Washington, DC, to her job in Silver Springs,
Maryland, a former welfare mother is happy to be
off welfare, but worries about the fragile child-
care arrangements for her four children under the
age of 14, and about whether she will be able to
keep her Medicaid card (two of her children have
asthma). As she emerges from welfare, this black

single mother joins the working poor. Graham insists that a welfare-reform policy which requires work should reward work. Women working at minimum wage and raising children need income subsidies.

7-21. Johnson, Beverly L., and Elizabeth Waldman. "Most Women Who Maintain Families Receive Poor Labor Market Returns." Monthly Labor Review 106 (December 1983): 30-34.

Women who head families are more likely to be employed or seeking employment than in the past, but their marginal earnings and high unemployment rate keep their families poor. Most employed women maintaining families work at full-time jobs in administrative support areas which are generally lower-paying or lesser-skilled jobs. On the average, black women have more dependent children and less education than white women, and black and Hispanic women who head households have lower median earnings, lower labor force participation rates, and higher unemployment rates than white women. The average income among families maintained by women is low, whether they are in or out of the paid workforce, and proportionately more live below the poverty line than do couple-headed families.

7-22. Kanter, Rosabeth Moss. "Work in a New America." Daedalus 107 (1978): 47-78.

The recession experienced in the seventies has created a more sober mood and a greater emphasis on national security, jobs, and work. However, the issues of work and conditions of work are perceived differently by different groups in the population. One remarkable labor trend is the high participation rate of women.

There is an identifiable undercurrent of changing cultural expectations about work, insisting that it be meaningful, along with new concern for individual rights and power.

7-23. Kemp, Alice Abel. "The Excluded Ones: Males and Females in Small or Very Segregated Occupations." Sociological Spectrum 3 (1983): 181-202.

Researchers who use occupational segregation as an explanation of the persistent male-female gap in earnings confuse it as a cause rather than as a consequence of the discrimination against women which is embedded in the organization of work. Granted that men and women do different work in our society, it does not necessarily follow that work done by women should almost always be worth less than work done by males. Jobs are divided according to desirability and stability of the work performed, with females and minority workers allocated to the less desirable and more unstable jobs. These jobs pay less and are more variable in the time worked. To secure equality in earnings, the structural characteristics of work, rather than the productivity characteristics of female and male workers, need to be examined.

7-24. King, Allan G. "Industrial Structure, the Flexibility of Working Hours, and Women's Labor Force Participation." Review of Economics and Statistics 60 (1978): 399-407.

Women's family responsibilities, especially child care, determine their ability to schedule their work. Their increased labor-force participation has to do with the greater flexibility in hours offered by the service sector as the economy shifted from an industrial to a service one.

Women flock to those industries where there is a
variability of hours. Mothers with preschool
children are a case in point. Industries with
flexible work hours will have significant impact on
women's labor-force activity.

7-25. Lipsitz, Joan. "The Economic Future of Girls and
Young Women." 1984. (ERIC
microfiche ED290818)

The economic future of women will be
determined by later marriage age, longer life
expectancy, higher divorce rates, and the
feminization of poverty. Lipsitz finds that most
women work outside the home, although girls
have limited employment goals. Girls do not
enjoy access to occupational options as do boys.
They lack on-the-job experiences and career
counseling. Societal messages to girls about work,
marriage and motherhood are mixed and
inconsistent; girls need constant counseling about
their roles and values.

7-26. McLennan, Barbara N. "Sex Discrimination in
Employment and Possible Liabilities of
Labor Unions: Implications of County of
Washington v. Gunther." Labor Law
Journal 33 (1982): 26-35.

In 1981, the Supreme Court found in
Gunther v. County of Washington that Congress
intended Title VII of the Civil Rights Act of 1964
to end all practices of sex discrimination in
employment. The author argues that Gunther
opens the door for women to sue employers for
sex discrimination on the basis of comparable pay,
and to sue labor unions as well, since women
would be referring to higher-paying (presumably
unionized) jobs, as they bring comparable pay
suits.

7-27. Maume, David J., Jr. "Government Participation in the Local Economy and Race-Based and Sex-Based Earnings Inequality." Social Problems 32 (1985): 285-299.

Although race and sex differences influence earnings, they do so differently. White men are rewarded for their job knowledge and training; white women are compensated in the labor market for length of time in job, total hours worked, occupational status, and union membership. When the government creates jobs locally, employment increases for black people and white women. When the government is a big purchaser of goods and services locally, these groups also gain in the labor market, probably due to affirmative action hiring policies. Government participation in the local economy had the greatest impact on the wages of black women.

7-28. Maurer, Harry. "When Being Unemployed Is What You Do (excerpts from Not Working: An Oral History of the Unemployed)." Ms., November 1979, pp. 87-90.

These excerpts from interviews of unemployed women indicate that they miss the monetary independence and sociability that working outside the home offers. They report fighting at home, crying jags, and overeating and depression. Women's experience of joblessness differs from men's. It is more widespread and severe, and women report more stress. Blue-collar women have the most problems coping with joblessness and receive the least help from anyone, including their spouses.

7-29.   Moen, Phyllis. "Measuring Unemployment: Family
Considerations." Human Relations 33
(1980): 183-192.

Most statistics on employment and well-
being focus on the individual, not on the family,
although unemployment of the head of household
certainly affects the economic well-being of the
family. The problem with the term
"unemployment" is that not all families with an
unemployed male head of household suffer
economically, and the term masks those outside
the labor force (discouraged workers, new
workers) and those who are involuntarily working
part-time or are underemployed. Women,
particularly, are among the group of discouraged
workers, and as heads of households are in the
out-of-the-labor-force category. It is essential for
policymakers to be aware that since the
unemployed female head-of-household is not a
category included as part of the unemployed, her
family's economic needs are not being analyzed.

7-30.   Moore, Sylvia. "The Short-Term Effects of Marital
Disruption on the Labor Supply Behavior
of Young Women." 1979. (ERIC
microfiche ED181277)

Marital disruption is no longer a rare
phenomenon, and the growing likelihood that it
will affect young families with children requires
clearly defined public policies to provide
employment training and economic assistance to
women who become heads of households.
Moore's statistical analysis found that of white
women who were above the poverty line before
divorce, 26 percent fell below it afterwards, as did
40 percent of the black women who became heads
of households. A major reason for the fall is the
low potential earning power of the female family
heads and the absence of income from sources
other than their own labor.

7-31. Nilsen, Sigurd R. "Recessionary Impacts on the Unemployment of Men and Women." Monthly Labor Review 107 (May 1984): 21-25.

In 1982, for the first time since 1947, the unemployment rate of men exceeded that of women (9.9 percent for men, 9.4 percent for women). Changes in the composition of the labor force and the recession of 1980-82 have contributed to the significant rise in the unemployment rate of men. The manufacturing sector experienced a substantial loss in its share of the labor force and was characterized by high unemployment rates, primarily affecting men, whereas the service industries have been the largest gainers and tend to have low unemployment rates (for women) even during recessions.

7-32. O'Kelly, Charlotte G. "The Impact of Equal Employment Legislation on Women's Earnings: Limitations of Legislative Solutions to Discrimination in the Economy." American Journal of Economics and Sociology 38 (1979): 419-430.

Although a strong legal basis now exists for equal opportunity in employment for females, their earnings have actually dropped in relation to that of males. This holds true even when experience on the job, lifetime work experience, and education are similar. Females are also still twice as likely as males to be below the poverty line. The impact of low female earnings may be of even greater significance today because of the increase in female-headed families. Equal opportunity legislation has not been sufficient to end economic sexism.

7-33.   Paulin, Beth, and Ray Marshall. "The Wages of
Women's Work." Society 22 (July/August
1985): 28-38.

Arguing in favor of comparable worth,
the authors point to the growing labor-force
participation of women and to the advantage
which accrues to employers who discriminate
against women and are able to employ a highly
educated and motivated workforce with limited
employment opportunities. However, the
American economy would be far healthier and
more efficient if women were paid what their
work is worth.

7-34.   Pearce, Diana. "Toil and Trouble: Women
Workers and Unemployment
Compensation." Signs 10 (1985): 439-459.

Most discussions about women's poverty
centers on replacing the male breadwinner's
income and does not focus on the failure of the
marketplace to provide sufficient income to all
workers, especially women. The majority of
women who head households work, yet one-fifth
of them are still poor. Over 90 percent of women
on welfare have worked or are currently working;
they turn to welfare when both their marriages
and the marketplace have failed to provide them
with sufficient income. Lacking unemployment
insurance, many women are forced into accepting
low wages and/or welfare, thus making their
position as workers more vulnerable.
Unemployment compensation is an extension of
the privileged male primary economic sector. It
does not require a means test, and it goes to male
breadwinners with more routinized work patterns.
Pearce recommends a single and universal system
of income support for the unemployed.

7-35. Portwood, James D., and Karen S. Koziara. "In Search of Equal Employment Opportunity: New Interpretations of Title VII." Labor Law Journal 30 (1979): 353-360.

Title VII of the Civil Rights Act as amended in 1972 guarantees equality in employment opportunity for all persons. The Supreme Court has ruled that intent to discriminate need not be shown for a case of discrimination to be made. The plaintiff need only show that an employment practice had a disparate effect on white males and any protected group. The Court also decided to defer to the Equal Employment Opportunity Commission (EEOC) administration's interpretations of the law. However, recent trends in the Burger Court have moved away from the EEOC guidelines in favor of greater latitude for businesses and employers.

7-36. Power, Marilyn. "From Home Production to Wage Labor: Women as a Reserve Army of Labor." Review of Radical Political Economics 15 (1983): 71-91.

Married women are moving into the labor market at ever-increasing rates. This movement has changed married women's economic role and created a reserve army of wage labor for the continued expansion of capitalism. No longer are women serving as a marginal labor force for capitalism; they have become part of the permanent labor force. This will tend to undermine the material base of patriarchy within the home. Women workers will become less a flexible segment of the labor force as they are forced by economic necessity to seek wage work and stay in the labor force.

7-37. Reskin, Barbara F., and Heidi I. Hartman, eds.
<u>Women's Work, Men's Work</u>.
Washington, DC: National Academy
Press, 1986.

The Committee on Women's
Employment and Related Social Issues studied the
differences in women's and men's working lives,
particularly differences in earnings and
occupations. The significance of sex segregation
for women includes lower wages, lower retirement
income, increased susceptibility to unemployment,
less access to on-the-job training, lower
occupational prestige, and increased job stress.
This report describes the research of a large
number of experts, as well as U.S. government
figures, on the extent of sex segregation in the
workplace, and includes explanations for the
segregation, as well as recommendations for
reducing it. Remedies include changes in job-
training programs and vocational education, along
with improved child care and flexible work
scheduling.

7-38. Saks, Daniel H., and R. E. Smith. "Youth With
Poor Job Prospects." <u>Education and
Urban Society</u> 14 (1981): 15-32.

Young people as a group are more likely
to experience unemployment and are paid less
when they do have jobs. Young women are being
prepared for employment in stereotypically female
occupations, jobs with lower pay and fewer
opportunities for advancement. Their wage rates
are lower than young men's, and their
unemployment rates are slightly higher. Their
problems are compounded by the baby boomers
swelling the labor market. Federal policies have
to be directed to the size of the population
entering the labor force, and the problems related
to race, sex, and other limiting conditions.

7-39. Sandell, Steven H. "Is the Unemployment Rate of Women Too Low? A Direct Test of the Economic Theory of Job Search." Review of Economics and Statistics 62 (1980): 634-637.

While the unemployment rate for women is considerably higher than that for men, the average duration of women's unemployment is shorter. Women who leave their jobs voluntarily experience shorter periods of unemployment than those who do not. There is little statistically significant difference between black and white married women in the sampling for duration of unemployment. Married women are better able to sustain longer job searches.

7-40. Smith, Joan. "The Paradox of Women's Poverty: Wage-Earning Women and Economic Transformation." Special Issue: Women and poverty. Signs 10 (1984): 291-310.

The significant growth in women's poverty can be attributed to more women having to depend exclusively on their own earnings or on welfare to support themselves and their children. Furthermore, the jobs available to women offer them little chance to climb out of poverty. In the seventies, the increased rate at which women became available for wage work enabled the development of the service economy. This sector presupposes and reinforces the view of women as a cheaper and more dispensable labor force, less dependent on their wages than are male workers. Women's poverty and continued economic dependency are the central operating premises of the service sectors which are the most rapidly expanding sectors of the U.S. economy.

7-41. U.S. Congress. Joint Economic Committee.
<u>Problems of Working Women</u>. 98th
Congress, 2nd Session. Washington, DC:
Government Printing Office, 1984.
(Y 4.Ec 7:W 84/7)

Witnesses discuss the lack of affordable
child care which hampers women's ability to enter
and remain in the workforce and to take
advantage of educational and training
opportunities. Other experts describe programs
designed to assist women on welfare make the
transition from welfare to work.

8 Comparable Worth and Pay Equity

Equitable pay for jobs of comparable worth and nondiscriminatory hiring or affirmative action represent strategies for achieving wage parity between women and men. Pay equity advocates seek not equal pay for equal work but equal pay for comparable work. Women are poor not because they do not work; they work, but they are paid less because less monetary value is placed on women's work. If women were paid comparably to men, i.e., nurses comparably to equally trained pharmacists, far fewer women and their children would be poor. Equal pay and antidiscrimination measures are not very effective because most women work at "women's jobs" and are therefore unaffected by them. In 1980, 57 percent of women working outside the home worked in female-dominated occupations. (Mark Aldrich and Robert Buchele, The Economics of Comparable Worth, Cambridge, MA: Ballinger, 1986, p. 150.)

The theory of comparable worth was introduced in the late seventies and more than 40 states have at least conducted comparable worth studies. This concept attacks the notion that men's work is more important and more skilled than women's work, and that women are secondary, dependent, intermittent workers. It rejects the premise of a separate and lower wage scale for women. Comparable worth seeks to establish compensation for the relative worth of jobs, based on levels of skills, education, effort, and responsibility required, regardless of the sex, race, or ethnicity of the job holder.

Both organized labor and the National Organization for Women support the principle of comparable worth and have exposed the anomalies in the relationship between women and wages. There seems to be no relationship between the skills involved in women's work and the wages paid. Regardless of the marketplace need for women's work (e.g., nurses), women's work is underpaid. The marketplace does not recognize women's skills, e.g., caring and facilitating skills, as skills worth compensating. And, lastly, women are not seen as being fully entitled to fair wages; they continue to be treated as secondary, dependent workers. (Roslyn L. Feldberg, "Comparable Worth: Toward Theory and Practice in the United States," Signs 10 [1984]: 311-328.)

Although the "equal pay for equal work" formula was worked out in the 1963 Equal Pay Act, comparable worth suits have been allowed under the broader provisions of Title VII of the 1964 Civil Rights Act. In 1981 the Supreme Court, while not upholding comparable worth, found Washington County guilty of intentional wage discrimination against its female prison guards whom it paid less than its male guards (County of Washington v. Gunther [452 U.S. 161]). Generally, there has been little success through the courts, and comparable worth advocates are seeking redress through state legislatures and collective bargaining.

Comparable worth advocates claim that wage hierarchies are lower for women not because of the natural laws of the marketplace but because of historical discrimination in the marketplace. These advocates seek a fair return on women's labor and the opening of traditionally higher paying male jobs to women. They recognize that a shift into jobs traditionally associated with men in the long run will not necessarily guarantee women better pay because these new jobs might, in turn, become subject to wage discrimination as they become pink-collared. For these reasons, comparable pay advocates are often also supporters of affirmative action. Along with placing pay equity within the scope of nondiscriminatory labor legislation, affirmative action legislation is needed to prevent occupational segregation. Marketplace segregation forces women and minorities into sectors of the economy which are then subject to unequal and discriminatory pay.

8-1. Aldrich, Mark, and Robert Buchele. <u>The Economics of Comparable Worth</u>. Cambridge, MA: Ballinger, 1986.

The authors begin with a historical survey of women's work in the United States. They examine recent efforts to implement comparable worth, survey leading theories of discrimination, and discuss the importance of occupational segregation in the comparable worth diagnosis of women's low earnings. Ending with an assessment of the impact of comparable worth on the distribution of earnings, they conclude that comparable worth wage increases would reduce wage inequality among all workers and also among women workers.

8-2. Bergmann, Barbara R. "Pay Equity: Surprising Answers to Hard Questions." <u>Challenge</u> 30 (May/June 1987): 45-51.

Discrimination exerts a powerful influence on the wages the market sets, and predominantly female occupations are paid less than predominantly male occupations. To end this discrimination, pay equity adjustments can be instituted based on job evaluations which assess the knowledge and skills required of each job. Job evaluation scores correlate well with male salaries but not with female. In pay equity plans the wage in a predominately female job is set equal to the wage of a predominately male job with the same job evaluation score. Raising women's wages in accordance with job evaluation throughout the economy might ease about one-third of the gap between men's and women's wage rates.

8-3. Bunzel, John H. "To Each According to Her
          Worth." Public Interest, Spring 1982, pp.
          77-93.

       In 1981, the city of San Jose, California,
settled with the American Federation of State,
County, and Municipal Employees (AFSCME),
thus ending the first municipal strike over
comparable worth. The agreed settlement sought
to narrow the salary gap between men and women
municipal employees. The author is unhappy
with the concept of comparable pay and says that
this is a new union tool to leverage better wages
for women through collective bargaining.

8-4. Burnett, Nancy. "Interview: 'Hardhat; Women on
          Comparable Worth'." Women's Rights
          Law Reporter 8 (1984-5): 83-93.

       This article includes five interviews with
women who left their traditionally female, lower-
paying jobs for nontraditional higher-paying male
jobs as coalminers, an electrician, and a salt
miner. Burnett asks how these women feel about
the higher salaries now being offered to younger
women in the jobs they left behind. By and large,
the women favor comparable worth and have
precise ideas for developing comparable worth
standards in their industries but think them
difficult to implement.

8-5. Cardenas, Gilbert. "Equity from an Economic
          Perspective." Research and Development
          Series no. 214B. 1981. (ERIC
          microfiche ED215158)

       Exploring the effect of income inequality
and the poor, Cardenas attributes discrimination
in the marketplace to the lack of education and
training for women and minorities. He believes

that vocational education needs to be more
responsive to the needs of the disadvantaged.

8-6. Cranston, Alan. "The Proposed Equity Act of
1985." <u>Labor Law Journal</u> 36 (1985): 131-
144.

The proposed Pay Equity Act of 1985 was
aimed at discriminatory wages paid to women,
one of the most pervasive forms of employment
discrimination. Senator Cranston (D-CA)
subscribes to both pay equity and comparable
worth. He says that the cost implications of pay
equity are vastly exaggerated, and he does not see
the federal government's vote as setting the wages
for all workers. He avows that the proposed
legislation would equalize wages for men and
women and would evaluate jobs on a
nondiscriminatory basis.

8-7. Duncan, Meryl L. "The Future of Affirmative
Action: A Jurisprudential Legal Critique."
<u>Harvard Civil Rights Civil Liberties Law
Review</u> 17 (1982): 503-553.

Affirmative action is defined as a public
or private program designed to equalize hiring
and admissions opportunities for historically
disadvantaged groups by taking into consideration
those very characteristics which have been used to
deny them equal treatment. Duncan argues that
the controversy surrounding affirmative action is
due to confusion over compensatory justice,
distributive justice, and social utility, and is further
complicated by affirmative action quotas on the
one hand and goals on the other. There is legal
consensus that at least blacks, Hispanics, Native
Americans, and women are entitled to affirmative
action. The principle of distributive justice
provides the strongest rationale for affirmative
action as it requires that benefits and burdens be

distributed in accordance with considerations of rights, deserts, merits, and the contributions and needs of the recipient.

8-8. Feldberg, Roslyn L. "Comparable Worth: Toward Theory and Practice in the United States." Special Issue: Women and Poverty. Signs 10 (1984): 311-328.

Comparable worth theory rejects the premise of separate and lower wages for women. Women's work, says Feldberg, is not worth less than men's, nor do women deserve lower wages. Comparable worth theory attacks the notion of the objectivity of the marketplace as determiner of wages; women's wages are impervious to the laws of supply and demand economies. The marketplace has historically paid women low wages. Comparable worth theory has the potential of ending market inequities for women by setting the value of women's work and giving women their right to earn equal wages.

8-9. Ferraro, Geraldine A. "Bridging the Wage Gap: Pay Equity and Job Evaluation." American Psychologist 39 (1984): 1166-1170.

Ferraro argues that the feminization of poverty emphasizes the need for pay equity and the end to occupational segregation. The promise of fair and decent wages for women requires vigorous enforcement of the laws such as Title VII and the Equal Pay Act. Unfortunately, Reagan's appointees on the Equal Employment Opportunity Commission turned a deaf ear to pay equity and complaints.

8-10. Fields, Diana. "Comparable Worth; the Next Step Toward Pay Equity Under Title VII." <u>Denver University Law Review</u> 62 (1985): 417-445.

The wage gap between men's and women's work continues, despite considerations of age, education and training, type of work performed, job history, and absenteeism. Comparable worth theory surfaced during World War II as women replaced men in the factories and employers sought to lower their wages. The author dismisses justification for discriminatory wages due to marketplace forces, pointing out that the resolution of the shortage of nurses was to import Philippine nurses rather than to raise wages, and concludes that comparable worth allows a uniform policy ending wage discrimination for women.

8-11. Floss, Frederick G. "Comparable Worth, Skill Groups and Market Interactions." <u>Women and Politics</u> 6 (1986): 25-42.

Comparable worth legislation seeks to address discrimination when individuals with the same skills are paid different wages. With the introduction of comparable worth initiatives, the pay differences within groups of skilled and unskilled female and male workers will disappear, but pay differences between the groups will not, as there is no free entry into the skilled classification, and it is likely that skilled wages will rise and unskilled wages will be lowered. The skilled female worker will be better off. The unskilled female worker will not be so fortunate.

8-12. Gee, Marguerite, and Denise Mitchell. "Women of Color and Pay Equity." National Committee on Pay Equity, Washington, DC. 1983. (ERIC microfiche ED253630)

      White women continue to earn at about 60 percent the wage rate of white men. Women of color, who have shown remarkable improvement in earnings ability, have reached and continued to earn at about 55 percent of white men's earnings. Despite this increase, women of color account for the highest percentage of female-headed households and families living in poverty. One explanation for this is women's occupational segregation in low-paying clerical and service work. Women of color are beginning to join white women in this sector as they move from blue-collar, operative work.

8-13. Hutner, Frances Cornwall. Equal Pay for Comparable Worth. New York: Praeger, 1986.

      Hutner begins with a discussion of the economic and legal issues of comparable worth, which is followed by a history of pay equity in the United States and abroad. The rest of the book consists of case studies of attempts to secure pay equity. Hutner notes that as more women work for wages, the question of pay equity grows more important to them and to their employers. This economic issue becomes a political issue and a question of control over who gets what and how much.

8-14. Kelly, Rita Mae, and Jane Bayes. "Symposium: Implementing Comparable Worth in the Public Sector: Theory and Practice at the State and Local Level" Policy Studies Review 5 (1986): 769-870.

In this symposium, six articles are presented which discuss adopting comparable worth as a policy for public sector employment. Legislative initiative is required at the state and local level because pay inequalities continue despite such federal legislation as the Equal Pay Act of 1963 and Title VII of the Civil Rights Act of 1964 (which made discrimination on the basis of sex illegal). Kelly and Bayes claim that successful implementation of pay equity policies in San Jose (California), Washington, Minnesota, and Iowa is due to coalitions between labor and women's groups.

8-15. Majors, Bruce Powell. "Comparable Worth: The New Feminist Demand." Journal of Social, Political and Economic Studies 10 (1985): 55-67.

Majors disagrees with comparable worth theorists. He does not believe that any one employer or employers set wages. It is the marketplace, the supply and demand for goods and services, that sets wages. Therefore he argues that comparable worth advocates would wreak havoc with the economy and wipe out other gains of the feminist movement.

8-16. Mann, Pamela. "Pay Equity in the Courts: Myth v. Reality." Special issue: Comparable Worth. Women's Rights Law Reporter 8 (1984-5): 7-16.

The author finds that, contrary to expectations in some sectors of public opinion, pay equity decisions have not had sweeping effects on women's wage-earning abilities. When dramatic proofs of systematic discrimination have been presented, such as in AFSCME v. Washington and Wilkins v. University of Houston, the courts have granted relief. But the courts have not generally prohibited wage discrimination against women and have refused to interfere with an employer's right to pay the lowest wage the market will bear. Mann concludes that although pay equity is an important tool in the struggle to eradicate the earnings gap between men and women, its effectiveness cannot yet be fully determined because of the courts' inactivity on matters of pay equity.

8-17. Paul, Ellen Frankel. Equity and Gender. New Brunswick, NJ: Transaction, 1989.

Paul, a scholar at the Cato Institute, begins with a chapter outlining the case for comparable worth implementation, including evidence for discrimination against women in the marketplace and a discussion of job evaluation schemes. She examines the case against comparable worth and then traces the history of comparable worth in the courts, the federal government, states, and collective bargaining and ends with a chapter on the philosophical considerations of the issue. She believes that comparable worth is retrogressive and that those who have a positive view of women's abilities should encourage them to compete in the marketplace.

8-18. Powers, Brian. "AFSCME v. Washington: Another
Barrier to Pay Equity for Women."
Harvard Women's Law Journal 9 (1986):
173-197.

Powers describes the reversal of
AFSCME v. Washington by the Ninth Circuit
Court as a setback to the gains made by the
acceptance of comparable worth theory by the
Equal Pay Act (1963), Title VII, 1964, and
Gunther (452 U.S. 161, 1981). The Court of
Appeals held in AFSCME that Title VII does not
prohibit employers from discriminatory pay scales
based on market rates. However, Gunther stands
and does allow comparable worth claims under
Title VII. State legislative action and
Congressional action are preferable to piecemeal
court decisions.

8-19. Ryan, Ellen M. "Comparable Worth: A Necessary
Vehicle for Pay Equity (for women)."
Marquette Law Review 68 (1984): 93-129.

That women suffer wage discrimination
when compared to men is indisputable. In
AFSCME v. State of Washington (578 F. Supp.
846 [W.1] Washington, 1983), a federal district
court allowed the theory's use in a wage
discrimination case. Ryan reviews the history of
such legislative initiatives as the Equal Pay Act
(1963) and Title VII of the Civil Rights Act (1964)
as amended by the Bennett amendment, Gunther,
and AFSCME, which advance the comparable
worth theory by ameliorating the undervaluation
of women's work.

8-20. Schonberger, Richard. J., and Harry W. Hennessey, Jr. "Is Equal Pay for Comparable Work Fair?" Personnel Journal 60 (1981): 964-968.

The Equal Pay Act of 1986 allows equal pay for equal work and the extended interpretation of equal pay for comparable work. The authors say that fair pay is a more complex issue than proponents of either pay equity or comparable worth would allow. By and large, the application of these concepts would benefit better-educated male and female professionals and technicians at the expense of unskilled unionized workers and semi-skilled tradespeople whose wages have been pushed up by unions.

8-21. Shattuck, Cathie A. "Sex-Based Wage Discrimination: A Management View." Denver University Law Review 62 (1985): 393-415.

Over the past 23 years, the courts have not been receptive to the doctrine of comparable worth, yet state and federal legislative developments indicate that employers will soon be subject to comparable worth statutes and should implement programs now to avoid liability. Currently, employers are not responsible for discriminatory wages resulting from either historical discrimination in the marketplace or societal attitudes which devalue women's work.

8-22. Stewart, Debra. "State Initiatives in the Federal System; the Politics and Policy of Comparable Worth in 1984." Publius 15 (1985): 81-95.

State and local governments have become active in advancing the comparable worth agenda. States act as laboratories as they compile data, perform job evaluation studies, enact pay equity legislation, and order compliance with pay equity provisions.

8-23. Thomas, Clarence. "Pay Equity and Comparable Worth." Labor Law Journal 34 (1983): 3-12.

Thomas, chair of the Equal Employment Opportunity Commission (EEOC), reviews the wage discrimination which women face, the remedies supplied by the Equal Pay Act of 1963 and Title VII of the Civil Rights Act of 1964, and the striking-down of the Bennett Amendment by the Supreme Court in the County of Washington v. Gunther (1981). Bennett allowed for sex-based discrimination if it were part of the seniority system.

8-24. U.S. Congress. House. Committee on Post Office and Civil Service. Pay Equity: Equal Pay for Work of Comparable Value. Parts I and II. 97th Congress, 2nd Session. Washington, DC: Government Printing Office, 1983. (Y 4.P 84/10:97-53/pts. 1 and 2)

Includes testimony from a variety of individuals on the issue of pay equity and comparable worth. Witnesses include representatives of labor unions and women's groups, as well as economists, some of whom describe the need for pay equity and others who argue against it. The appendices contain publications of numerous organizations concerned with the issue, along with several bibliographies.

8-25. U.S. Congress. Joint Economic Committee.
Women in the Work Force: Pay Equity.
98th Congress, 2nd Session. Washington,
DC: Government Printing Office, 1984.
(Y 4.Ec 7:W 84/8)

This hearing was held to consider the
problems and remedies of wage discrimination. It
includes testimony on a report by the National
Research Council that there is "considerable
discrimination in pay; that job segregation is
pervasive and not entirely the result of women's
choices; that women are concentrated in low-
paying jobs that are low paying at least partly
because women do them" (p. 4). The document
includes testimony of economists on the pros and
cons of the concept of comparable worth, of the
National Committee on Pay Equity on the costs of
wage discrimination and the need for pay equity,
as well as a reprint of their publication "The Wage
Gap: Myths and Facts."

9 Reaganomics

During the seventies, it became popular to declare that the War on Poverty had been won, that income transfer and anti-poverty efforts had worked to guarantee economic opportunity and an adequate standard of living to all but the most disadvantaged Americans. This accomplished, resources could be shifted away from social programs and the poor toward the needs of the private sector for greater capital investment. The evidence with regard to poverty shows otherwise. Statistically, the overall reduction in poverty for families during the seventies was from 12 percent of the United States population in 1969 to 11.6 percent of the population in 1979.

In 1981, Congress passed the first major budget of the Reagan Administration, the Omnibus Budget Reconciliation Act (OBRA), which not only cut back social programs but also significantly reduced the number of newly arrived members of the middle class. This act included among its many provisions the first major reforms since 1967 of Aid to Families with Dependent Children (the principal program providing cash assistance to needy children and their custodial parents in single-parent families, and in half the states, to two-parent families in which the breadwinner is unemployed). OBRA cut not only AFDC, but also block grants that funded domestic violence programs, day care and family-planning services; housing programs; food stamps; and the Legal Services Corporation; and eliminated CETA (the Comprehensive Employment and Training Act). These were all programs that had a direct impact on lower-income women and their children.

Although a slowdown in the growth rate of spending on social welfare programs had begun under President Carter, the drastic cuts in welfare instituted by Reagan were new. In keeping with a basic tenet of the Reagan Administration, the cuts represented a rejection of using the federal government and its programs to move people into the mainstream. AFDC, over time, became the program through which the government sought to modify the behavior of the poor in order to move poor families out of poverty. However, conservatives like George Gilder insisted that AFDC promoted welfare dependency for generations of families and worked antipoor beliefs into both OBRA and The Family Support Act of 1988. In his 1982 State of the Union address, President Ronald Reagan asserted that he had "...inherited a system in which valuable resources were 'going not to the needy but to the greedy,' [and] the President vowed that his economic program would 'protect the needy while it triggers a recovery that will benefit all Americans.'" (Margaret Burnham, "The Great Society Didn't Fail," Nation 249 [July 24/31, 1989], p. 123.)

The changes in AFDC under OBRA were part of an overall plan to cut government costs and to shift responsibility for social programs to state and local government, and to reduce welfare costs and caseloads by concentrating benefits on the "truly needy," those entirely dependent on welfare. The thrust of the changes in the program was directed at the small percentage of AFDC families with earnings, less than 12 percent in 1981, removing them from the rolls so that by 1982 only 5 percent had earnings, and the remaining working recipients received lower benefits than before OBRA.

Though the feminization of poverty began before President Reagan took office, his policies exacerbated it, since women and children were disproportionately affected by cuts in means-tested programs. Under OBRA, the welfare rolls were reduced and case loads were lightened because program changes restricting entry discouraged continued participation in the program. Unequivocally, women were much worse off financially than they had been in the pre-OBRA period. Of those who were

terminated from AFDC and thereby lost their eligibility
for Medicaid, nearly one-fourth of the women and one-
third of their children had no health insurance coverage in
January 1983. Average incomes dropped between 6 and
21 percent. In New York City, looking at income one
month before and one month after OBRA, the number of
families below the poverty line almost doubled. Studies of
the psychological impact of the cuts under OBRA reported
that women's sense of well-being declined when they could
no longer combine work and welfare. Women did this
using AFDC in much the same way that other workers use
unemployment insurance, as a stopgap measure, and
OBRA took this option away.

9-1. Albeda, Randy, and others. <u>Mink Coats Don't
Trickle Down: The Economic Attacks on
Women and People of Color</u>. Boston,
MA: South End Press, 1988.

Chapters are entitled "Scarcely Allocating
Resources," "Are You Better Off Today...?,"
"Reaganomics and Racial Inequality," and
"Women and Children Last." The authors argue
that poverty has become feminized because "the
family is increasingly doing without its principle
source of funds--men", and that the government
has not made up the difference. They contend
that conservative economic policy is about family
policy as well. Ironically, while the conservative
social agenda aims to restore the male-headed
nuclear family, women are entering the labor
force as men are losing their traditional blue-
collar jobs. Women continue to earn less than
men, however; they are held back by the
Reaganites' reliance on market forces. The
authors recommend public policies that increase
women's employment opportunities and wages,
provide adequate support for childrearing, and
provide adequate income support.

9-2. Aldous, Joan. "Cuts in Selected Welfare Programs:
The Effects on U.S. Families." <u>Journal of
Family Issues</u> 7 (1986): 161-177.

This article presents measures of hunger,
health programs, and job training for women and
children family members during the Reagan years
from fiscal 1982 through fiscal 1986. Hunger-
prevention programs such as school lunch and
breakfast programs and food stamps program
were cut. The measures indicate that there has
been a pronounced increase in hunger in the
United States. Since 1980, more women and
children have been subject to hunger and
malnutrition, and reductions in health programs
such as neonatal care have led to increased infant

mortality rates. In the area of job training, those who need it most--youth ready to leave home--are being ignored. It was expected that because of the recession there would be an increase in the number of people who would be receiving aid. Instead, Aldous found fewer people receiving aid and an increase in social problems like hunger, sickness, and joblessness.

9-3. Block, Fred, and others. <u>The Mean Season: The Attack on the Welfare State</u>. New York: Pantheon, 1987.

At a time when there is a simultaneous attack on the welfare state and a business offensive against labor, the American economy is shifting away from an industrialized base, which will cause greater dislocations, unemployment, and need for the cushion of social programs. The marketplace will emerge as the organizing principle governing the lives of poor and working people. This is seen clearly in workfare programs, where mothers are coerced into particular jobs at whatever wages the employer chooses to offer. These essays are intended to provide an ideological framework for democratic resistance to market domination. Francis Fox Piven and Richard A. Coward reject the conservative claim that the welfare system has worsened poverty and family instability. Fred Block challenges current views that social welfare costs are sapping the strength of the American economy and that austerity is a precondition for further economic growth. Barbara Ehrenreich argues that the New Right has attacked public support for welfare.

9-4. Breckenfeld, Gurney. "Has Reagan Hurt the
Poor?" <u>Fortune</u>, January 24, 1983, pp. 77-
78+.

Although the Reagan Administration has
made a fundamental shift in its treatment of the
poor and the rich via income tax cuts, the
hullabaloo greatly exceeds the amount of change.
Reagan has reversed nearly 50 years of increasing
federal efforts to redistribute income, arguing that
the programs do not help the poor and that they
cost too much. The big tax cuts of 1981 are
returning more dollars to high-income than to
low-income households. Three recessions and the
feminization of poverty cloud an assessment of the
impact of cuts in taxes, food stamps, and Aid to
Families with Dependent Children.

9-5. "Caucus Readies For Assault on 'Reaganomics' in
1982." <u>Jet</u>, October 15, 1981, pp. 5-7.

The Congressional Black Caucus warns of
a growing conservative movement threatening the
quality of black life in America. Budget cuts in
social programs and expanding holes in the
societal safety net will hit the black community the
hardest. Black organizations must be mobilized
and the black vote shown at the polls. At present
both Democrats and Republicans ignore it or take
it for granted.

9-6. Cusick, Theresa. "A Clash of Ideologies: The
Reagan Administration versus the
Women's Educational Equity Act." 1983.
(ERIC microfiche ED266079)

Under Reagan, the federal government is
backing off from ensuring opportunity for
education. Nowhere is this more apparent than in
the weakening of the Women's Educational
Equity Act of 1978 (WEEA). Reagan has

continued to press Congress to withhold funding
from the program, which seeks to address the
special problems of minority and disabled women
and to increase the participation of women in
scientific and technical fields.

9-7. Eisenstein, Zillah R. "The Patriarchal Relations of
the Reagan State." Special Issue: Women
and Poverty. Signs 10 (1984): 329-337.

The Reagan Administration's antifeminist
policies are aimed at the destruction of the
welfare state and the dismantling of social services
in order to advance the conservative notion of the
traditional nuclear family. Cutbacks in social
welfare programs will eliminate the new middle
class of welfare administrators, especially white
and black women and black men. Reagan's
antiwomen policies are continued by opposition to
affirmative action, job training, abortion rights,
and equal pay.

9-8. Erie, Steven P., Martin Rein, and Barbara Wiget.
"Women and the Reagan Revolution:
Thermidor for the Social Welfare
Economy." In Families, Politics, and
Public Policy: A Feminist Dialogue on
Women and the State, pp. 94-119. Edited
by Irene Diamond. New York: Longman,
1983.

The authors argue that the gender gap
must be examined in terms of Reagan's welfare
and budgetary policies, since women constitute the
vast majority of human services workers and
welfare family heads. While many factors have
contributed to the feminization of poverty, "large
numbers of women are trapped in poverty by the
complex interplay between federal welfare policy
and the low-wage labor market" (p. 100). The
authors postulate two results of the Reagan

cutbacks: many women may be forced out of
social welfare jobs and into low-wage private
sector jobs and others will be forced out of private
sector jobs into workfare programs.

9-9. Fishman, Joelle. "'Gender Gap'--A Big Hurdle for
Reaganism." Political Affairs 63 (April
1984): 2-8.

Long before he entered the White House,
Reagan was unpopular with women. The
increasing number of women at the polls has the
potential of playing a critical role in the election.
The majority of these women are wage earners
engaged in trade union struggles. The intensity of
these struggles can be measured by Reagan's
systematic undermining of the civil rights gains of
the past decade, including affirmative action. The
Reagan Administration is anticommunist and
antiworking class, and the confines of the
capitalist bourgeois democracy make it hard to
battle for women's representation.

9-10. "From Women: Sterner Verdict on Reagan." US
News and World Report, May 18, 1981, p.
48.

Women leaders are skeptical of Reagan
and his social welfare policies. Congress scores
no better. Women particularly criticize Reagan's
efforts to reduce the government's role in
everyday life.

9-11. Harrington, Michael. "Reagan: Taking Food from
the Poor." Mother Jones,
September/October 1981, pp. 50-52.

The Reagan program is a conscious effort
to reverse antipoverty programs of the sixties
which reduced poverty in that decade and well

into the early seventies. Reagan cut $3 billion
from food programs (including food stamps,
school breakfasts, summer lunches). He claims he
is eliminating abuse, but his actions show an
indifference to the traditional family life he says
he advocates.

9-12. Hawkins, Augustus. "A Jobs Program for the
       1980's." Social Policy 14 (1983): 32-36.

Rep. Hawkins (D-CA) coauthored the
Full Employment and Growth Act of 1978 with
Sen. Hubert Humphrey (D-MN). The purpose of
the Humphrey-Hawkins Act was to translate into
reality the right to a job by setting goals to reduce
unemployment and inflation and by implementing
specific job related programs. Reaganomics has
subverted the Humphrey-Hawkins Act by
increasing unemployment to fight inflation and by
refusing to target youth, minorities, and women
for job programs. The federal budget should be
used to promote full employment, full production,
and economic investment. Targeted programs
must include housing, jobs, income support, food,
and health programs.

9-13. Kittle, Robert A., and Avery, Patricia A. "Behind
       Reagan's Trouble with Women Voters."
       U.S. News and World Report, May 31,
       1982, p. 51.

Women voters are voicing less support
than men for President Reagan. The gender gap
is estimated at 10 percentage points in political
support. Although some explain this gap by
Reagan's antiabortion and anti-Equal Rights
Amendment stands, the authors believe that
Reagan's national security stance and his
economic program are to blame. More women
than men are fearful that Reagan's defense
buildup will result in war, and more women are

skeptical that the Reagan program of budget cuts
and tax reduction will generate prosperity without
hurting the poor and the elderly, the majority of
whom are women.

9-14. Palmer, John L., and Isabel Sawhill, eds. The
Reagan Experiment: An Examination of
Economic and Social Policies under the
Reagan Administration. Washington,
DC: Urban Institute, 1982.

The Urban Institute saw the Reagan
Administration experimenting with domestic
policies in ways that were as significant as the
New Deal. In this volume, they monitor and
interpret significant shifts in domestic policy as the
Reagan counter-revolution seeks to limit the role
of government. With a commitment to expand
America's defense capability and reduce tax
burdens, there was a reduction in domestic
spending and a retrenchment and reformation of
social programs. Reagan's socioeconomic policies
shifted responsibility to state and local
governments, relied on the private sector, and
reduced benefits to individuals. The Reagan
social revolution did not turn back the clock very
far, however. For example, the narrowing of the
social safety net rejected the idea that the federal
government has a commitment to assist the poor
regardless of the reasons for their poverty, which
led to a substantial cut in food stamp and AFDC
spending. Left intact, though, was support for the
"deserving poor."

9-15. Palmer, John L., and Isabel V. Sawhill, eds. The
Reagan Record: An Assessment of
America's Changing Domestic Priorities.
Cambridge, MA: Ballinger, 1984.

This is the Urban Institute's second book
assessing the consequences of Reagan's desire to

limit the role of the federal government (see #9-14 above). Seeking to restore prosperity, reduce the size of the government, and increase national security spending, the administration focused on the economy and the budget and curtailing domestic programs. Reagan reduced or eliminated benefits for those groups he believed ought to rely on work and other means of private, rather than public, support. The Reagan Administration expected private charities to supplant the federal dole, businesses to provide a healthy economy, and state governments to fill in. The President was only partially successful in his full-scale retreat from the welfare state. He failed to reform spending, tax, and regulatory policies and financed middle-class entitlements and tax preferences by increasing the budget deficit.

9-16. Piven, Frances Fox, and Richard A. Cloward. The New Class War. New York: Pantheon, 1982.

The authors describe the Reagan Administration's 1981 cuts in social spending, arguing that "the income-maintenance programs are coming under assault because they limit profits by enlarging the bargaining power of workers with employers." Women, especially those who work in the service sector, are particularly vulnerable.

9-17. "Reaganomics Kills." Progressive 47 (April 1983): 10.

Some statistics do not lie. The infant mortality rate in Detroit matches that of Honduras; a 15 percent increase in the unemployment rate means 320 more Americans will commit suicide during the year. The Reagan response? Cutting social program spending including Medicaid and other health programs.

9-18. Sarri, Rosemary C. "Federal Policy Changes and the Feminization of Poverty." Special Issue: Toward a Feminist Approach to Child Welfare. Child Welfare 64 (1985): 235-247.

The economic condition of American women is deteriorating; they now head 50 percent of all poor households. The Reagan Administration significantly altered welfare programs as it reduced benefits, resources, guarantees, costs, and caseloads, all reductions in major social programs serving the working poor and women. With the passage of the Omnibus Budget Reconciliation Act (OBRA) in 1981, federal policy increased poverty in the United States.

9-19. Sarri, Rosemary C. "The Impact of Federal Policy Change on the Well-Being of Poor Women and Children." In Families and Economic Distress: Coping Strategies and Social Policy, pp. 209-231. Edited by Patricia Voydanoff and Linda C. Majka. Newbury Park, CA: Sage Publications, 1988.

Sarri points out that while programs serving needy families made up less than 10 percent of federal expenditures, between 1981 and 1985 they sustained 30 percent of all budget cuts. The Reagan Administration accepted the thesis about the dangers of welfare dependency and reduced AFDC and other programs for poor women. Sarri studied terminated recipients in Michigan and Georgia and found increased hardship caused by the Omnibus Budget Reconciliation Act (OBRA). She believes that the new emphasis on workfare will not alleviate poverty among women and children.

9-20. Schafran, Lynn Hecht. "Women and the Reagan
Administration: Promises and Realities."
USA Today 111 (July 1982): 9-12.

Having repudiated the ratification of the
Equal Rights Amendment, President Reagan
appointed Sandra Day O'Connor to the Supreme
Court. Despite Reagan's professed commitment
to ending discrimination against women, analysis
of his administration reveals a continuing denial of
women's rights and women's ability to participate
in society as equals. He urged elimination of the
$122 per month minimum Social Security benefit
whose recipients are primarily women. He cut
welfare, funding for day care, food stamps, and
job training, and denied women the gains of
previous decades.

9-21. Siciliano, C. A. "In Aid of the Working Poor: the
Proper Treatment of Payroll Taxes in
Calculating Benefits under the Aid to
Families with Dependent Children
Program." Fordham Law Review 52
(1984): 1171-1208.

Aid to Families with Dependent Children
(AFDC) was intended as an antipoverty
entitlement program to provide minimum
subsistence to impoverished children and their
adult caretakers. AFDC has also provided
assistance to working families on the brink of self-
sufficiency. Historically, government regulations
have favored the applicant. However, the
Omnibus Budget Reconciliation Act of 1981
sought to reduce federal AFDC spending and
targeted the working poor for cuts in order to
maximize the funds available to the "truly needy".
Most severely hit were families with female heads
who were thrown back onto welfare.

9-22. Uehara, Edwina S., Scott Geron, and Sandra K.
        Beeman. "The Elderly Poor in the
        Reagan Era." <u>Gerontologist</u> 26 (1986):
        48-55.

        Analysis of state and federal public
assistance cutbacks under the Reagan
Administration indicates that the elderly have
fared better than the nonelderly poor. Although
the cash benefits have been protected, cutbacks in
medical care and food stamp programs have
affected their health and well-being. As they are
less able to compensate through work for their
losses and less able to mobilize other informal or
institutional resources, the impact of the federal
cuts on the elderly is more serious than it appears.

9-23. U.S. Congress. House. Committee on the Budget.
        <u>Effects of the Administration's Fiscal
        Year 1984 Budget on Children and
        Youth</u>. 98th Congress, 1st Session.
        Washington, DC: Government Printing
        Office, 1983. (Y 4. B85/3: B85/16).

        Includes Reagan Administration
testimony on changes to AFDC resulting from the
Omnibus Budget Reconciliation Act (OBRA) of
1989 and the Tax Equity and Fiscal Responsibility
Act (TEFRA) of 1982. The laws required that all
family income and resources be considered in
determining need and strengthened work
requirements for recipients. Testimony from
representatives of groups such as the Food
Research and Action Center refutes
Administration claims that the safety net is intact.

9-24. U.S. Congress. House. Committee on the Budget.
Overview of the Administration's
Entitlement Policies. 98th Congress, 1st
Session. Washington, DC: Government
Printing Office, 1983. (Y 4.B 85/3:En
8/3)

Committee hearing held to conduct an
overview of the Reagan Administration's
entitlement policy, especially as it relates to
Medicare and Medicaid. Includes the testimony
of Marian Wright Edelman of the Children's
Defense Fund (CDF, pp. 98-139) on the effects of
budget cuts on children, including the loss of
Medicaid coverage, preventive health services,
food stamps, and free and reduced-price lunches.
The CDF also submitted an analysis of the cost
effectiveness of primary and preventive health
care, including prenatal care.

9-25. U.S. Congress. House. Committee on Ways and
Means. Effects of the Omnibus Budget
Reconciliation Act of 1981 (OBRA)
Welfare Changes and the Recession on
Poverty. 98th Congress, 2nd Session.
Washington, DC: Government Printing
Office, 1984. (Y 4.W 36:WMCP 98-33)

A microsimulation report that attempts to
sort out the relative importance of the recession,
budget reductions, particularly in AFDC, and
other factors on increases in the poverty rate.
The report concludes that the recession had a
stronger effect than OBRA on the increase in the
overall poverty rate. However, OBRA had a
stronger impact on the poverty rates both among
children and among members of female-headed
families.

9-26. U.S. Congress. House. Committee on Ways and Means. <u>Families in Poverty: Changes in the "Safety Net"</u>. 98th Congress, 2nd Session. Washington, DC: Government Printing Office, 1984. (Y 4.W 36:WMCP 98-37)

Results of a study which examined the experiences of a typical AFDC family (mother and two children) in 1980 and 1984 in order to illustrate the impact of Reagan's cuts in social spending. State-by-state analysis showed that poor families were unable to maintain their standard of living, that families with no wages lost 8-9.7 percent of their disposable income, and that single-parent families among the working poor lost between 14.5 and 22.5 percent of their income. All loss of income was caused by spending cuts and tax law changes.

9-27. U.S. Congress. House. Committee on Ways and Means. <u>Poverty Rate Increase</u>. 98th Congress, 1st Session. Washington, DC: Government Printing Office, 1984. (Y 4.W 36:98-55)

Hearings held to determine reasons for the increase in the poverty rate from 11.4 percent in 1978 to 15 percent in 1983. Includes a report from the Institute for Research on Poverty at the University of Wisconsin on "Macroeconomic Conditions, Income Transfers, and the Trend in Poverty" (pp. 49-65) which concludes that economic growth is unlikely to have an effect on poverty rates among nonaged female-headed families. Also includes testimony from David Stockman, the director of the Office of Management and Budget (pp. 213-264 and 325-335) who argues that the 1981-82 budget and tax reforms did not devastate the safety net.

9-28. U.S. Congress. House. Select Committee on Children, Youth, and Families. Safety Net Programs: Are They Reaching Poor Children? 99th Congress, 2nd Session. Washington, DC: Government Printing Office, 1986. (Y 4.C 43/2:Sa 1)

A report, primarily statistical, that describes the safety net designed to protect the 12.5 million American children who lived in poverty in 1986. The report details national and regional trends in poverty 1979-1984. Based on an analysis of participation in AFDC, Head Start, WIC (Special Supplemental Food Program for Women, Infants and Children), the report concludes that "the record growth in poverty among children has not been accompanied by increased availability of key safety net programs" (p. v).

9-29. Wodarski, John S., and others. "Reagan's AFDC Policy Changes: The Georgia Experience." Social Work 31 (1986): 273-281.

The Omnibus Budget Reconciliation Act of 1981 (OBRA) sought to reduce the costs of welfare and Medicaid by terminating benefits of top earners. In Georgia, it was found that mothers could not make it and had to turn to welfare. Their lives were made harder. These women became ill, anxious or depressed, reapplied for benefits, and asked the father of their children for more support. Only two percent asked for a hearing of their case. AFDC did not prove to be a work disincentive for the group surveyed.

9-30. Zinn, Deborah K., and Rosemary C. Sarri. "Turning Back the Clock on Public Welfare." Special Issue: Women and Poverty. <u>Signs</u> 10 (1984): 355-370.

By 1982, the Bureau of the Census reported that 15 percent of the population of the U.S. was living in poverty. This was a trend that was accelerated by the decrease in welfare aid to women and children under Reagan's Omnibus Budget Reconciliation Act (OBRA) of 1981, reversing the previous trend under Nixon and Carter of extending public benefits and expanding federal responsibility. The authors studied female heads of households whose benefits were terminated under OBRA and found them to be educated with few dependents, and yet they were unable to provide for the basic needs of their children. OBRA exacerbated and reversed the decline in poverty rates.

10 Poverty and Women of Color

Twenty years after the Kerner Commission (Report of the National Advisory Commission on Civil Disorder, Washington, DC: Government Printing Office, 1968) found that white racism and the continued polarization of American society caused the urban race riots of the sixties, Richard Bernstein wrote in the New York Times (February 29, 1989, p. B8, col. 1) that the gap between blacks and whites still exists. He quotes Professor William Julius Wilson of the University of Chicago, a sociologist and author of The Truly Disadvantaged:

> In fact, there are three different groups. There's a black middle class that has experienced gradual progress. There's a black working class that has had difficulty holding its economic position because it's been vulnerable to de-industrialization. And there's a black underclass that's slipping further and further behind the rest of society.

Three times as many blacks as whites live in poverty; overall black median income is 57 percent that of whites, and the gap has widened slightly over the last 10 to 15 years. During the Reagan years, writes Bernstein, there has been "a tacit acceptance ... of unequal conditions for blacks."

Poverty among blacks has also been closely linked to the increase in female-headed households. (William P. O'Hare, "Poverty in American: Trends and New Patterns,"

Population Bulletin 40 [1985]: 19-20.) Approximately 50
percent of black families are headed by women. These
families experience greater rates of poverty and a variety
of health and socio-economic problems associated with low
income than do their white counterparts. In 1987, black
female-headed families had weekly earnings of $284, white
female-headed families earned $329, while white married-
couple families earned $647. (Statistical Abstract of the
United States 1989, Washington, DC: Government Printing
Office, 1989, Table 667.) The large number of female-
headed families is due in part to the large numbers of
black mothers who never marry. The divorce rate among
black families is twice that of white families, due in part to
high unemployment rates among low-income black
husbands and fathers. The public welfare system, as
presently structured, does little to encourage poor families
to maintain strong ties. (Joyce A. Ladner and Ruby
Morton Gourdine, "Intergenerational Teenage
Motherhood: Some Preliminary Findings," Sage 1 [1984]:
22-24.)

Some scholars disagree with the concept of
feminization of poverty and its application to black women.
In "Has Poverty Been Feminized in Black America?"
(Black Scholar 16 [March/April 1985]: 14-49), Linda
Burnham says that the theory selects the factor of gender
as the cause of poverty among women and disregards
analysis of class and race in addition to disregarding the
extent of poverty among black men. "The conditions of
the Black community in the U.S. are completely framed by
the fact that the U.S. class structure is thoroughly
racialized." The fact is, she says, the female poor are
disproportionately composed of racial and ethnic minority
women.

10-1. Amott, Teresa. "Race, Class, and the Feminization of Poverty." Socialist Politics No. 3 (April 1985): 5-11.

The increased number of women and children in poverty is due to a change in family structure, with the number of single-parent families growing more rapidly than two-parent families, and to an erosion since 1972 of government programs which provide income to these women. As a backlash to the black movement of the sixties, continued racist stereotyping played a crucial role in undermining support for welfare programs in the seventies and eighties. Reforms must make government programs recognize the economic rights of all citizens.

10-2. Ball, Richard E. "Marital Status, Household Structure and Life Satisfaction of Black Women." Social Problems 30 (1983): 400-409.

After reviewing the literature which has described the black family structure as weak and inferior, Ball asserts that blacks, especially black women who head households, have developed alternatives to the traditional nuclear family, incorporating relatives and unrelated individuals, thus extending their resources. He finds that the impact on life satisfaction for black women is not greatly influenced by the absence or presence of a husband, nor does family augmentation greatly influence life satisfaction of black female heads of households.

10-3.   Bianchi, Suzanne M., and Reynolds Farley.   "Racial
                Differences in Family Living
                Arrangements and Economic Well-
                Being."   Journal of Marriage and the
                Family 41 (1979): 537-552.

                Reflecting on the Moynihan Report of
        1965 (see #10-30), which cited female headship
        and illegitimacy as causes for the deterioration of
        black families and the fundamental weakness of
        black communities, the authors note that there
        was a hidden assumption that a normal household
        is a working male supporting a dependent wife
        and children.   The authors conclude that the
        Moynihan Report was wrong; family instability is
        not restricted to blacks but is paralleled in the
        white community.   Updating Moynihan's report,
        the authors find that although similar trends typify
        blacks and whites, changes in family living
        arrangements have been more substantial among
        black families, producing a widening of racial
        differentials in family status and affecting their
        economic well-being.

10-4.   Brewer, Rose M.   "Black Women in Poverty: Some
                Comments on Female-Headed Families."
                Signs 13 (1988): 331-339.

                Industrial capitalism has historically
        sustained and protected white families with state
        labor legislation that has not protected the black
        family from racism and economic discrimination.
        The American economy has not been shaped by
        concerns for preserving black family life.
        Consequently, some blacks have been unable to
        integrate work with family life and they experience
        under-employment and unemployment in urban
        labor markets.   Increasingly, women have
        depended on a combination of work and welfare
        as heads of households, since they are
        systematically excluded from the advanced
        capitalist order; the flip side of their

impoverishment is the declining economic status
of black men.

10-5. Brimmer, Andrew. "Prosperity Among Black
            Women." Black Enterprise 15
            (December 1984): 45+.

The analysis of American incomes focuses
on the high incidence of poverty among blacks.
However, there is a considerable degree of
prosperity among black women, particularly
among those with marketable skills. In the case
of married women who work, black women
contribute more to their families' incomes than do
white women, and as individuals, black women
with above average incomes are well represented.
In 1983, more than two million black women had
incomes over $30,000 as compared to 449,000
black men.

10-6. Brischetto, Robert R., and Paul A. Leonard.
            "Falling Through the Safety Net: Latinos
            and the Declining Effectiveness of Anti-
            Poverty Programs in the 1980's." 1988.
            (ERIC microfiche ED294946)

Concentrating on Latinos in the
Southwest, this report finds that Latinos are
falling through the safety net that government
agencies are supposed to provide. Poverty among
Latinos has increased in the eighties, the hardest
hit being children, while poverty among the
elderly has been declining due to Social Security.
Latinos who work have been pushed into poverty
by jobs that pay wages below the poverty line to a
greater degree than have blacks or whites.
Female-headed families were hardest hit by the
decline in antipoverty programs during 1979-1983.
In 1979, two out of five female-headed Latino
families with children were lifted out of poverty by
all cash and noncash transfers of public assistance

programs; by 1983, the proportions helped out of poverty by these programs had declined to one in five.

10-7. Burnham, Linda, and others. "Has Poverty Been Feminized in Black America?" Special Issue: Black Women and Feminism. Black Scholar 16 (March/April 1985): 2-49.

Theories about the feminization of poverty mask the unequal burden of poverty. White women do not suffer poverty at the rates that black women do. In 1981, more than half (52.9 percent) of black female-headed households lived in poverty compared to 27.4 percent of white female-headed households. Class and race, not gender, are the significant factors determining who is poor, causing intergenerational poverty and perpetuating the circumstances which leave minorities bearing the brunt of poverty.

10-8. Claude, Judy. "Poverty Patterns for Black Men and Women." Black Scholar 17 (September/October 1986): 20-23.

The black community is now experiencing the feminization and racialization of poverty. Black women have made some economic gains, but have not gained equality with other groups and have suffered from erosion of government aid. Family structure does not account for their poverty. Black men are also experiencing increasing joblessness and poverty, and many of them become permanently unemployed. All of these phenomena must be included in an interpretation of black poverty.

10-9. Comer, James P. "Single Parent Black Families."
Crisis 90 (December 1983): 42-47.

The understandable rejection by the black
community of the Moynihan Report in 1965
should not prevent current reappraisal of the
report, as the black community is reeling from
poverty, family disintegration, and high rates of
single-parenting. The author traces the
development of the black family, the prosperity of
stable families, and the plight of poor, destabilized
families. The phenomenon of single-parent
families is enmeshed in, and is a product of,
complex powerful historical and contemporary
social forces and requires a coordinated, multi-
focus approach between black and white
communities at every level.

10-10. Darity, William A., Jr., and Samuel L. Myers, Jr.
"Does Welfare Dependency Cause
Female Headship? The Case of the
Black Family." Journal of Marriage and
the Family 46 (1984): 765-779.

Darity and Myers investigate whether
there is an economic motivation for the dramatic
increase in black female-headed households, that
is, do these women choose welfare over marriage?
They find no statistical evidence to support the
economic motivation theory for choosing welfare
nor the belief that welfare causes female headship.
They believe that possible explanations lie in these
young women having been reared in female-
headed families where the nuclear family model
has never taken root. The growing incidence of
black female-headed families reflects the
deepening problem of sheer survival for black
people in America, a population
disproportionately without technical skills and
resources to provide stable family arrangements.

10-11. Darity, William A., Jr., and Samuel L. Myers, Jr.
"Public Policy and the Condition of Black
Family Life." Review of Black Political
Economy 13 (1984): 165-187.

American families today, especially black
families, suffer from disruption, with poor black
women forming households to a disproportionate
degree and educated middle-class black women
remaining childless. The authors allow the claim
that welfare has contributed in part to the current
crisis in black families and the growth of female
headship. Public policy has disrupted the
traditional roles of women in the home and men
as breadwinners, and the decline in black family
life is an erosion of the traditional structure.
Home life can be bettered by an alliance of the
black women who are raising families and the
black men who are being left out.

10-12. Edelman, Marian Wright. Families in Peril: An
Agenda for Social Change. Cambridge,
MA: Harvard University Press, 1987.

As head of the Children's Defense Fund
(CDF), the author believes that the best way to
help poor black children is to show that white
children are similarly affected. In this book, she
explores the connections between poor female-
headed households, male joblessness, and poverty
and concludes that "the key to bolstering black
families, alleviating the growth in female-headed
households, and reducing black child poverty lies
in improved education, training, and employment
opportunities for black males and females" (p. 14).
Edelman argues that loss of cohesiveness in the
black community has resulted in a lack of hope
for those left behind, and that black self-help is
important but not enough. Pointing out that
poverty is the number-one killer of American
children in the eighties, she outlines preventive
strategies, including the CDF's program for

prevention of adolescent pregnancies, points out
some successful Great Society programs of the
Johnson era, describes AFDC reforms, and ends
with an exhortation for social change.

10-13. Erie, Steven P. "Public Policy and Black Economic
Polarization." Policy Analysis 6 (1980):
305-317.

Since the mid-sixties, the black
community has been polarized between a
developing middle class and an urban underclass
dependent on public assistance. Government
policies leading to public employment, public
assistance, and worker training seem to foster this
duality in the labor market. While black poverty
prior to the sixties primarily reflected low
agricultural wages in the South in households
headed by men, by the late sixties, the majority of
low-income black families living outside the South
were headed by women and maintained by
welfare. The large-scale movement of blacks into
the public labor market in tandem with welfare
programs has institutionalized the polarization in
the black community and made it a public sector
community, with one part the recipients of
welfare, the other, the providers.

10-14. "Falling Behind: A Report on how Blacks Have
Fared under Reagan." Journal of Black
Studies 17 (1986): 148-172.

This report provides an analysis of data
from government agencies and the Urban Institute
which shows that the economic status of black
Americans deteriorated in the first four years of
the Reagan Administration. The report includes
statistics on income, poverty, unemployment, and
the impact of tax policies and federal budget cuts,
which disproportionately affected black
Americans.

10-15. Farley, Reynolds. "After the Starting Line: Blacks and Women in an Uphill Race." <u>Demography</u> 25 (1988): 477-495.

The continuing high rates of black unemployment are due to shifts in employment and industry and the social and economic roles of women. Farley suggests that changes in family structure that occurred among blacks are a leading indication of what may happen to white families; that as black women's educational and occupational opportunities increase along with their economic gains, marriage becomes less necessary. If the earnings of white women equal or surpass white men, white families may soon resemble black families, and the majority of white children will be born to unmarried women and raised in families headed by women, possibly living below the poverty line.

10-16. George, Hermon, Jr. "Black America, the 'Underclass' and the Subordination Process." <u>Black Scholar</u> 19 (1988): 44-54.

George explores racism and the continuing economic subordination of blacks. He disagrees with the ethnicity theorists (Glazer and Moynihan) and sees racism as triumphant over pluralism. The concerns of African-Americans are being excluded from the public agenda, and George argues that the system is willing to elevate individuals but never blacks as a group.

10-17. Gordon-Bradshaw, Ruth H. "A Social Essay on Special Issues Facing Poor Women of Color." <u>Women and Health</u> 12 (1987): 243-259.

Women of color experience racism, sexism, prejudice, discrimination, poverty, poor health, and low educational achievement; all of which compromise the quality of their lives. Poverty is a pervasive theme in the lives of women of color, who are often concentrated in inner cities. They are often over-qualified for the jobs they get and see less return for their investment in schooling than white women, whose jobs often reward them with pension funds or other social benefits. Black women rely on welfare or social security. They are disenfranchised when it comes to health care and suffer needless deaths from cancer, heart disease, drugs, homicides, childbirth, etc. Women of color must demand full equality in education, employment, and housing, and they must require policymakers to provide child care, school-based health programs, quality health care and human service programs.

10-18. Gwartney-Gibbs, Patricia A., and Patricia A. Taylor. "Black Women Workers' Earnings Progress in Three Industrial Sectors (Comparison of 1960 and 1980 Earnings From U.S. Census Public Use Samples in Core, Periphery and Government Work Sectors)." Sage 3 (1985): 20-25.

Scholars have become disenchanted with the neoclassical economic theory of human capital where investments in knowledge and training are rewarded in the competitive labor market. They are recognizing evidence of discrimination and segregation and structural features of the economy which provide different and discriminatory access to achievement for blacks and women and limit their earnings. Greater employment in the public sector and enforcement of affirmative action and comparable worth will enhance the wages of minority groups.

10-19. Hesse-Biber, Sharlene. "The Black Woman Worker: A Minority Group Perspective on Women at Work." <u>Sage</u> 3 (1986): 26-34.

Although black women workers share many bonds with all working women, in their disadvantaged position in the labor market, they suffer the additional burden of racial discrimination. They work because of economic necessity and the continued economic vulnerability of black men. They are believed to have superhuman qualities as economic mainstays and matriarchs of the family. But, although black women have always had high rates of labor-force participation, they are employed in the least desirable occupations, and their income and status is lower. They have high rates of unemployment, and more black families headed by women live below the poverty line.

10-20. Jewell, K. Sue. <u>Survival of the Black Family: The Institutional Impact of U.S. Social Policy</u>. New York: Praeger, 1988.

Jewell argues that "policies, procedures, and assumptions underlying social and economic programs in the 1960's and 1970's contributed to the disintegration of the black two-parent and extended families, and to an increase in black families headed by women" (p. ix). She examines the social programs of the sixties and seventies, then assesses their impact on black families. She describes the reformulation of social policy that took place during the Reagan years: the new federalism, the shift from collective to private responsibility, mandated workfare, and unfair budget cuts. She points out that conservative social policy did lead to some changes in black families, including revitalization of mutual-aid networks and increased visibility of the black church. Jewell concludes with recommendations for a social policy for black families.

10-21. Jones, John Paul, III. "Work, Welfare, and Poverty Among Black Female-Headed Families." Economic Geography 63 (1987): 20-34.

     Jones presents a statistical analysis of whether welfare benefits programs and/or labor market characteristics explain the different rates of poverty in different states. His analysis shows that welfare is more attractive to black female heads of households in those states where black women are clustered in low-wage clerical jobs and services. Furthermore, unemployment among black women has an effect on the poverty-welfare relationship; in areas where there are lower rates of unemployment, there are lower rates of reliance on public assistance.

10-22. King, Allan G. "Labor Market Racial Discrimination Against Black Women." Review of Black Political Economy 8 (1978): 325-335.

     Analyzing the commonly held belief that black women have achieved economic parity, King asserts that black women have advanced primarily in public-sector jobs and that these advances have been made by the youngest cohorts. Black women, even the most highly educated, continue to suffer discrimination. Both black and white women's earnings are falling further behind men's earnings.

10-23. Kondracke, Morton M. "The Two Black Americas." New Republic, February 6, 1989, pp. 17-20.

The black middle class is prospering, but it feels tenuous in its economic position, and the black underclass is growing. There are three schools of thought about social policy with regard to the underclass: the conservative Charles Murray's welfare school, the liberal William J. Wilson's structural unemployment/social isolation school, and Glen Loury's culture of poverty school. What President Bush will do with his "thousand points of light" remains to be seen.

10-24. Lacayo, Carmela G. "Income Fact Sheet on Older Hispanics." 1983. (ERIC microfiche ED261137)

Lacayo outlines the magnitude of the incidence of poverty among elderly Hispanics. Based on 1980 census data, Hispanics over 65 are more than twice as likely to be poor as Anglos. One out of every four older Hispanics was classified as poor by the Census Bureau. Poverty is particularly widespread among older Hispanic women, whose the poverty rate is more than twice that of elderly Anglo women. Lacayo considers the rates of poverty among elderly Hispanics to be far greater than reported by the Census Bureau due to the undercounting of Hispanics and the exclusion of poor people living in households which are not classified as poor.

10-25. Ladner, Joyce A. "Black Women Face the 21st Century: Major Issues and Problems." Black Scholar 17 (September/October 1986): 12-19.

Black women continue to suffer from the burdens of racism, sexism, and poverty. Despite

the achievement of those who have been trained
and educated, the majority of black women earn
less than black and white men and white women.
The feminization of poverty and increasing rates
of adolescent pregnancy have eroded the strengths
of black females, whose economic position was
weakened under Reagan. The decline in marriage
rates for blacks is attributed to high rates of
unemployment, imprisonment, and the lessening
of social pressures for women to marry.
Transformation of the market economy from
industrial to service has not benefitted blacks on a
large scale. Ladner advocates pregnancy-
prevention programs and transitional job
programs for welfare mothers.

10-26. McGhee, J. D. "A Dream Denied: The Black
          Family in the Eighties." Urban League
          Review 6 (1983): 193-218.

          The emergence of the black middle class
in the sixties still leaves about 70 percent of all
black families with low or very low incomes. The
massive shift in federal spending from social
programs to national defense, tax reforms for
corporations and the wealthy, and the New
Federalism which shifts the administration and
payment of social programs to the states together
constitute an assault on the poor. They mean that
people will go hungry, be cold, and lack shelter.
In the long run, they will relegate a large number
of potential workers to the hopelessness and
despair of a lifetime of unemployment and poverty
and will undermine the majority of black families.

10-27. Malveaux, Julianne. "The Economic Interests of Black and White Women: Are They Similar?" Review of Black Political Economy 14 (1985): 5-27.

Malveaux challenges the women's agenda which seeks to have policies aimed at female-headed households. These policies are inadequate because the issues of poverty in the black community go beyond women to high rates of male under-employment and unemployment. Theorizing about the feminization of poverty tends to blur differences between women of color and white women. Black women work more than white women and earn less. Black women experience greater occupational segregation in clerical jobs. A policy agenda for black women must include full employment and fair wages, reduction of racial discrimination in labor markets, and social support for single mothers, and must focus on both their gender and racial interests.

10-28. Malveaux, Julianne. "Race, Class, and Black Poverty." Black Scholar 19 (May/June 1988): 18-21.

Questioning the rapidity with which the term underclass has taken hold, Malveaux wonders why Lockheed Corporation was not called underclass when it was bailed out. She asserts that "underclass" is less an economic term than a behavioral term and the issue is not the existence of an underclass, but poverty. It is not the behavior and morality of the poor that ought to be examined but that of an economic system that generates neither opportunity nor equality but perpetuates poverty as it maintains its reserve army of the unemployed. She argues that the poor are sentenced to a life of minimum wage-slavery, with workfare for relief, and are called

upon to exhibit a morality exceeding that of other
citizens.

10-29. Maxwell, Joan Paddock. "No Easy Answers:
Persistent Poverty in the Metropolitan
Washington Area." Greater Washington
Research Center, Washington, DC. 1985.
(ERIC microfiche ED269490)

Census data from 1980 confirms that
poverty in the Washington, D.C. area is
concentrated among blacks, especially among
black female-headed families. The percentage of
black adult males not working increased from 27
percent to 41 percent in the seventies. Poverty
among black children is increasing. It is not likely
that these families will be able to pull themselves
out of poverty through employment because they
are either too young or too old or poorly
educated. Poor uneducated black female heads of
households have a particularly hard time earning
their way out of poverty. Income support appears
to be the only short-term solution.

10-30. Moynihan, Daniel Patrick. The Negro Family: The
Case for National Action. U.S.
Department of Labor. Office of Policy
Planning and Research. Washington, DC:
Government Printing Office, 1965.

Although published in 1965, and therefore
outside the scope of this bibliography, Moynihan's
report is included because of its importance to the
debate about poverty in the black community.
This controversial report includes statements on
the "tangle of pathology" such as "...the Negro
community has been forced into a matriarchal
structure which, because it is so out of line with
the rest of American society, seriously retards the
progress of the group as a whole, and imposes a
rushing burden on the Negro male and, in

consequence, on a great many Negro women as well." Moynihan's basic premise is that black family structure of matriarchy is becoming more acceptable as it becomes less economically viable.

10-31. Murray, Sandra Rice, and Daphne Duval Harrison. "Black Women and the Future." <u>Psychology of Women Quarterly</u> 6 (1981): 113-122.

Black women will continue to face harsh economic conditions and will see their labor-force participation continue at its present rate. Unemployment rates will remain devastating despite increasing levels of educational achievement. Consequently, black women will turn towards the church and Africa for opportunities for advancement and growth.

10-32. Nichols-Casebolt, Ann. "Black Families Headed By Single Mothers: Growing Numbers and Increasing Poverty." <u>Social Work</u> 33 (1988): 306-313.

The growing number of black families headed by females is due in large part to the economic insecurity of black males. The dissolution of the black family structure is the cause of poverty among these families, and the increasing numbers of black female-headed families can be attributed to a growth in welfare benefits and erosion of traditional values. However, welfare payments, particularly to black single mothers, do little to alleviate poverty. Further, the majority of black single mothers do not depend on welfare for the largest share of their income. Unless black men are able to earn an adequate income, black women may have little choice but to parent alone and to assume total financial responsibility for their children.

10-33. Oliver, Melvin L., and Mack A. Glick. "An Analysis of the New Orthodoxy on Black Mobility." Social Problems 29 (1982): 511-523.

The new orthodoxy claims that racial discrimination is no longer a problem, that the evidence presented by intergenerational occupational mobility shows blacks have caught up with whites since the sixties, and, consequently, economic programs aimed at achieving equality are no longer needed. By examining occupational mobility patterns back to 1962, the authors challenge this orthodoxy and find that the gains were not significant compared to white men and that present rates of black mobility will not bring them equality with whites. If blacks had similar mobility to whites, it would take them two generations to achieve parity. Further, racial criteria is still an important factor in differentiating mobility patterns in the labor market, and race-conscious public policies which attempt to remedy past inequities are valid.

10-34. Pearce, Diana. "The Feminization of Ghetto Poverty." Society 21 (1983): 70-74.

The changing demographics of the ghetto, with men moving out and leaving women and children behind, reflect the long-term structural shifts both in the labor market and in marriage and childbearing practices. The trends which are characterized as the feminization of poverty are appearing more strongly in the black community. During the seventies, the number of poor black families maintained by men declined by 35 percent, while the number maintained by women increased by 62 percent. In the course of one decade, black female-headed families increased from about one-half to three-fourths of all poor black families. The greater rates of poverty among women can be traced to two causes:

women bear the economic burden of raising
children, and, because of sex discrimination,
occupational segregation, and sexual harassment,
women who seek to support themselves and their
children through paid work are at a disadvantage
in the labor market. Black women experience
further disadvantages associated with race and are
more dependent on welfare than white women.

10-35. "Poor Black Men, Women Hit by Depression Most
Often." Jet, October 1, 1981, p. 24.

Poor black men and women are the most
frequent victims of depression. Women are twice
as likely as men to be depressed. The highest
levels of depression are among those adults
earning less than $8500 a year.

10-36. Rank, Mark R. "Racial Differences in Length of
Welfare Use." Social Forces 6 (1988):
1080-1101.

Do black and white women remain on
welfare for different periods of time, and is the
social pathology associated with the black family
greater than that of whites of similar economic
status? A sampling of Wisconsin's welfare
recipients found that black women were on
welfare a median of 45.2 months; white women,
21.6 months. Yet, if education, previous
employment, number of children and age were
taken into account, and if racial differences in the
length of welfare dependency are eliminated, then
black and white women behave identically in their
use of welfare. However, these variables do come
into play, and black women appear more reluctant
to get off public assistance. Having fewer
opportunities, not race, accounts for black
women's greater dependency on public assistance.

10-37. Rodgers, Harrell R., Jr. "Black Americans and the
Feminization of Poverty: The Intervening
Effects of Unemployment." Journal of
Black Studies 17 (1987): 402-417.

Black Americans are suffering the highest
rates of poverty of any subgroup. The poverty
rate for black Americans in 1983 was 35.7 percent,
the highest since 1967, and three times the poverty
rate for white Americans. The major change that
has occurred within the poor black population has
been the increase in female-headed households.
Higher divorce and separation rates, increases in
single-parenting, and numerical imbalances
between the sexes account for the feminization of
poverty. This crisis is compounded by the fact
that a large percentage of the black male
population is suffering from unemployment and
that poverty in the black community will remain
high as long as black men have serious financial
and employment problems.

10-38. Rodriguez, C. E. "Hispanics and Hispanic Women
in New York State." 1984. (ERIC
microfiche ED263227)

Hispanic women who head households in
New York State are the most in need, having 43
percent of the comparable income of white
women heads of households. They are less well
represented in the labor force, have lower-paying
dead-end jobs and are employed in the public
sector less frequently than black or white women.
Fertility rates indicate that Hispanics will be the
fastest-growing ethnic population in New York
and the country. Rodriguez urges greater
employment in the public sector and provision of
preschool education, and calls for greater
differentiation in analysis between whites and
Hispanics.

10-39. Simms, Margaret C. "Black Women Who Head
Families: An Economic Struggle."
Review of Black Political Economy 14
(1985-86): 141-151.

A family's economic position is related to
its composition. Families headed by women have
lower incomes than families headed by men or
married couples. Black families with female
heads have lower incomes and higher poverty
rates than any other type of family. This trend of
families being headed by women is on the
increase, especially in the black community where
female-headed households are in the majority.
Government programs in the eighties have
reduced public assistance while emphasizing work
incentives and increased paternal support. This
has not resulted in a decent standard of living for
women and their children. More aggressive
policies are needed to provide child care, job
training, and adequate transfer payments.

10-40. Simms, Margaret C. "Slipping Through the Cracks:
The Status of Black Women." Special
issue. Review of Black Political Economy
14 (1985-1986): 5-300.

This special issue presents the views of
the symposium on the economic status of black
women. Employment, education, health, single-
parent families, women in the Third World, and
policy implications are addressed. Simms and co-
editor Julianne Malveaux conclude the symposium
by emphasizing the need for full employment at
fair wages with adequate benefits, reform of the
tax structure, affirmative action, emphasis in the
federal budget on programs to ensure community
survival, child care, improved educational access,
health care, and employment and training
programs.

10-41. Smith, James P., and Finis Welch. "Race and Poverty: A Forty-Year Record." American Economic Review 77 (1987): 152-158.

Reviewing census data back to 1950, the authors found that there has been a 40-year record of blacks' economic progress. However, in the seventies, the accelerating breakup of black families, the rising rates of black unemployment, and a slowdown in economic growth contributed to the downslide of black progress. Female-headed families did not share in this economic progress, and their income did not keep up with overall economic growth. The increasing concentration of the black poor in female-headed families has stemmed the long-term reduction in black poverty.

10-42. Stewart, James B. "Some Factors Determining the Work Effort of Single Black Women." Review of Social Economy 40 (1982): 30-44.

How are the labor-market activities of never-married teenage black mothers affected by their decision to raise their children? 1970 data reveals that where there is an extended family, the young black woman who keeps her children can work. Older unmarried black mothers work more than younger mothers. Generally, the impact of childbearing on the work effort of young never-married black females varies. There is a positive correlation between work effort and simultaneous school attendance. Social welfare policies concerned with child care should not rely solely on commercial day-care facilities but should consider subsidizing households and encouraging greater use of the extended family.

10-43. Trader, Harriet Peat. "Welfare Policies and Black Families." Social Work 24 (1979): 548-552.

The American welfare state does not guarantee the welfare of black families. The welfare system, controlled and financed by a majority society, has very different interests than the minority it is supposed to help. Aid to Families with Dependent Children was never developed to help the whole family. It was built around the child and consequently disrupts the family. Black communities serve as conduits of colonialism, where the public welfare dollar is transferred out of the community to landlords, merchants, loan sharks, etc.

10-44. U.S. Congress. House. Committee on the Budget. Women and Children in Poverty. 98th Cong., 1st Session. Washington, DC: Government Printing Office, 1984. (Y 4 B85/3: W84)

Includes testimony from Eleanor Holmes Norton, a law professor at Georgetown University, on the black family, particularly the increase in female-headed households. Harriette McAdoo, who, along with Diana Pearce, is responsible for the conceptualization of the feminization of poverty, also submitted a summary of her research on single black mothers, particularly on the levels of stress experienced by those women.

10-45. Wilkenson, Margaret B., and Jewell Handy Gresham. "The Racialization of Poverty." Nation, July 24/31, 1989, pp. 126-132.

The authors argue that the "feminization of poverty is real, but the racialization of poverty is at its heart." Black women and their children are poor partly because black men have a high unemployment rate. Furthermore, the recent welfare reform measures that will force women to work do not take into account the problem of child care and the lack of rewarding jobs. Wilkenson and Gresham point out that proposals for national service for youth would require poor youths to volunteer either for national service or the military in order to earn federal money for college. Along with welfare, the national service plan would create a pool of cheap labor (young black women) and a pool of young black men for military service.

11 Older Women and Poverty

America's elderly population is growing, and women are a large majority of the elderly. Although social security benefits, private pension plans, and medical insurance programs like Medicare have helped to reduce poverty among the aged, women make up a disproportionate percentage of the elderly poor. Seventy-two percent of all poor Americans over 65 are women. (U.S. Congress. House. Select Committee on Aging, The Quality of Life for Older Women: Older Women Living Alone, Washington, DC: Government Printing Office, 1989, p. 2.) Minorities are at greater risk of becoming poor in old age. Blacks and Hispanics represent the poorest groups of aged Americans. In 1982, the Senate reported that 36 percent of aged blacks and 38 percent of aged Hispanics lived in extreme poverty. Minority women fared even worse, with 80 percent of aged black women and 50 percent of older Hispanic women in poverty compared to 20 percent of all aged women. (Women's Equity Action League, Facts on Social Security, Washington, DC: WEAL, 1985.)

Older women as a whole have lower average incomes than older men. In 1985, the average monthly social security benefit for women was $399 as compared to $521 for men. (U.S. Department of Health and Human Services, Monthly Benefit Statistics Program Data: Old-Age Survivors, Disability, and Health Insurance, Washington, DC: Government Printing Office, 1985.) The social security system discriminates against women; see Chapter 12 for information on inequities in the system. Elderly women are at a disadvantage because of their

patterns of paid employment. They pay twice, first in
lower income, then in lower retirement benefits.
Furthermore, women receive no pay for their work in the
home, and women who work outside the home often
interrupt their careers for childbearing and childrearing.
Women are concentrated in lower-paying occupations; they
face discrimination and lower wages. Many elderly women
may be caring for elderly parents or be forced into poverty
when their husbands are institutionalized. In many states
a spouse must be poor or spend down in order to receive
Medicaid benefits, and women are more likely than men
to have an institutionalized spouse.

Older women also face health problems. They
are less likely than men to have private health insurance to
supplement Medicare, and they are more likely to live
alone with no paid help for medical heath problems. They
also face the physical and mental stresses of caring for an
ailing spouse or elderly parents.

It is not the fact that women live longer that
causes poverty in old age, nor are they isolated from their
communities nor abandoned by their families. It is the
accumulation of their life choices which reflect second-
class status that makes them poor: their interrupted job
careers due to childbearing and rearing and family caring,
their seasonal and part-time employment which is evidence
of other primary demands on their time as well as their
acculturation to dependency and secondary wage labor.
When her economic position is no longer masked by the
earnings of the primary male earner, the elderly woman is
left in poverty, without the economic resources to make
her comfortable and to reflect her long life as a laborer in
both the paid and unpaid labor market.

11-1. Abu-Laban, Sharon McIrvin. "Women and Aging: A Futurist Perspective." Psychology of Women Quarterly 6 (1981): 85-98.

The author believes that the life of elderly women will be easier in the years 2000-2025. Unlike the current elderly population, they will not be the products of traditional sex-role socialization and gender-specific opportunities. However, the conservative religious trends in current American society might counter this brighter future for the elderly as they resurrect right-wing Protestant fundamentalism which not only underscores traditional authoritarianism in American society but advocates traditional and subordinate roles for women.

11-2. Arendell, Terry, and Carroll Estes. "Unsettled Future: Older Women, Economics and Health." Feminist Issues 7 (1987): 3-24.

The poverty experienced by older women is not a result of old age but of lifelong patterns of discrimination in the marketplace and of women's role as caregivers. These factors determine the economic status of women and affect their health status. There is no publicly financed health coverage for the nondisabled mid-life and older woman younger than 65 unless she is destitute or qualifies for Medicaid. Displaced homemakers are unlikely to have private health insurance. Divorced women are unlikely to have any kind of health insurance. Lack of money and the presence of preexisting medical conditions preclude access to private health insurance for many unmarried mid-life and older women. Governmental policies, particularly retrenchment in the reductions in federal health programs, undermine the position of older women.

11-3. Borker, Susan R., and Julie Loughlin. "Implications of the Present Economic Position of Middle-Aged Divorced and Widowed Women: Another Generation of the Elderly in Poverty." 1979. (ERIC microfiche ED183432)

Interviewing women in mid-life (age 39-53), the authors found that their economic prosperity is illusory. As the number of female-headed households increases, women, especially black women with the sole responsibility for childrearing, will see a declining economic status as they age because they will be unable to accumulate assets. Despite continued investment in education and job training and affirmative action programs, it is unlikely that women will approach income equality with men of the same age.

11-4. Coe, Richard D. "Longitudinal Examination of Poverty in the Elderly Years." Gerontologist 28 (1988): 540-544.

This study examined experiences of the elderly poor from a longitudinal perspective, using data from the Michigan Panel Study of Income Dynamics, and examined the probability of the elderly poor escaping poverty. For an elderly person during the first three years of poverty, the exit probabilities were high. After this period, there was little likelihood of escape. In general, both black and white elderly either escaped from poverty relatively quickly or they did not escape at all. Women who became poor averaged 5.9 of their elderly years in poverty, compared to 3.9 years for elderly men.

11-5. Cubillos, Herminia L. "Los Ancianos: The Aging of the Hispanic Community, a Preliminary Demographic Profile." Project Anciano. 1987. (ERIC microfiche ED289940)

Although Hispanics are a young population, the Hispanic elderly are among the most economically, physically and emotionally vulnerable. The data presented in this study shows that the Hispanic elderly population is growing rapidly and is concentrated in California, Texas, New York, and Florida. They are the least educated elderly subgroup and the least likely to receive social security benefits. Hispanic females are poorer than Hispanic males, which is consistent with the thesis of the feminization of poverty. The poverty rate for Hispanic elderly is twice as high as the rate for white elderly.

11-6. Dressel, Paula L. "Gender, Race and Class: Beyond the Feminization of Poverty." Gerontologist 28 (1988): 177-180.

Theories about the feminization of poverty distort the importance of race and social class, especially among the elderly. Racial stratification and oppression are primary features of the political economy. Feminist analysis fails to recognize that racial-ethnic women share political interests with racial-ethnic men and that class is an important factor as well. Dressel concludes that it is necessary to abandon concern over women's disproportionate impoverishment.

11-7. Estes, Carroll L., Lenore Gerard, and Adele Clarke. "Women and the Economics of Aging." <u>International Journal of Health Services</u> 14 (1984): 55-68.

The poverty women experience in old age is a result of gender discrimination which they have experienced their entire lives as wives and workers. Older women experience ageism, sexism, and specific employment policies (e.g., retirement) which undermine their continued work. Access to income maintenance and health care is denied the near poor; there are some 30 million people in the U.S. who lack health care coverage. Women's social role as family caregivers and their interrupted careers in the labor market do not secure for them significant health or retirement benefits.

11-8. Gantz, Paula. "Our Golden Years - You Should Live So Long!" <u>Lilith</u> 10 (Winter 1982-1983): 6-9.

Twenty percent of the Jewish population in New York City is 65 years or older. Approximately 25 percent of the Jewish elderly live at or near poverty levels. Most of these elderly are women whose savings are ravaged by inflation and the structure of the social security system. As laws are currently structured, old people must pauperize themselves before they can qualify for many government programs and services.

11-9. Heen, Mary L. "Sex Discrimination, Mortality Tables, and Pensions: Improving the Economic Status of Older Women." <u>Women and Health</u> 11 (1986): 119-131.

Retired women workers continue to suffer the harsh economic effects of double discrimination: inadequate pension coverage as a result of their low wages and coverage based on sex-based actuarial tables. Retired women receive lower pension benefits than men who have been similarly employed. This practice was overthrown by the Supreme Court ruling in <u>Arizona Governing Committee v. Norris</u> which held that Title VII of the Civil Rights Act of 1964 prohibits the use of sex-based actuarial tables to calculate sex-differentiated employee retirement benefits in employer-sponsored plans only.

11-10. Holden, Karen C. "Poverty and Living Arrangements Among Older Women: Are Changes in Economic Well-Being Underestimated?" <u>Journal of Gerontology</u> 43 (1988): 22-27.

Reviewing census data for 30 years (1950-1980), Holden investigated whether poverty rates for women have not fallen as they have for other elderly populations because elderly women live alone in increasing numbers. She found that poverty rates for elderly women did decline and would have declined more if they had not lost their spouses. However, the oldest among the elderly who live alone and do not, as a rule, share in the prosperity of other family members, saw the least decline in their poverty rate.

11-11. Jackson, Jacquelyne Johnson. "Aging Black Women and Public Policies." <u>Black Scholar</u> 19 (May/June 1988): 31-43.

After attacking the racist stereotyping of elderly black women, Jackson emphasizes the position of women who have been affected by both racism and sexism. The reasons for their poverty are insufficient participation in the labor force, low wages, insufficient pension coverage, and having little or no savings. Important reforms to address their poverty should include full federal funding of Medicaid and alternative forms of social security, transforming it into a true social insurance program.

11-12. Minkler, Meredith, and Robyn Stone. "The Feminization of Poverty and Older Women." Gerontologist 25 (1985): 351-357.

The elderly are the fastest-growing minority in the United States and, if they are women they suffer from the triple jeopardy of being old, poor, and female. The structural roots of the feminization of poverty are planted in the common law tradition assuming women's dependence and continue in the sexual division of labor, reflected in the dual labor market economy which underpays women. The budget cuts of the Reagan Administration continue to hit hardest at the elderly and the poor, most of whom are women, thus graying the feminization of poverty.

11-13. Moon, Marilyn. "Poverty Among Elderly Women and Minorities: Changing Domestic Priorities Discussion Paper." 1985. (ERIC microfiche ED296045)

Contrary to much of the reported literature, the rate of poverty among the elderly has not decreased; rather the poverty rate for the rest of the population has increased. Women are a growing percentage of the elderly poor, reflecting their increase in numbers relative to men. Poverty among the minority elderly is due to their below-average wages. Elderly women need improvements in pension coverage and medical costs; minorities need improved opportunities for earnings, pensions, and savings.

11-14. Morgan, Leslie A. "Economic Change at Mid-Life
Widowhood: A Longitudinal Analysis."
Journal of Marriage and the Family 43
(1981): 899-907.

In cross-sectional studies, widowhood has
been found to have a negative association with the
financial well-being of women. Results of the
cross-sectional analysis replicate previous
ambiguous findings which support the hypothesis
that mid-life widows tend to suffer economically.
No significant decline was found in women's
income or financial well-being after the death of
their spouses. Without a spouse's income, widows
relied on their own earnings and social security
benefits. A probable explanation for not finding a
dramatic shift in the well-being of the widows is
that many were already poor.

11-15. Morgan, Leslie A. "Work in Widowhood: A Viable
Option." Gerontologist 20 (1980): 581-
587.

Older women are often encouraged to
return to work as an option for alleviating their
poverty. Here, Morgan evaluates this option and
finds it limited, as many widows already work.
Morgan finds that few women who have not
worked begin paid employment when widowed
because they lack skills and often face
discrimination in a tight job market.

11-16. Mudrick, Nancy R. "Income Support Programs for
Disabled Women." Social Science Review
57 (1983): 125-136.

There is growing focus on programs for
the disabled with a view towards reducing them
and reducing the number of women who may
qualify. While the social science literature focuses
on disabled men because most of the Social

Security Disability recipients are men, women
report more disabilities and more severe
disabilities than men. Since the aging population,
where more disabilities occur, is
disproportionately female, the disabled are
disproportionately elderly women. Gaps in
coverage are likely to continue because reforms in
disability programs are often linked to previous
work patterns, which for women are not as stable
or as remunerative as men's employment.

11-17.   Muller, Charlotte. "Income Supports for Older
         Women." Social Policy 14 (1983): 23-31.

Recognizing the economic problems of
older women in society (brought about by sex-
typed job histories with lower earnings and
resulting lower social security earnings), Muller
proposes solutions which would not penalize
women for their poverty nor cause them to lose
their independence. Since the annual median
income for women over 65 is only $400 above the
poverty line, she proposes raising supplemental
Security Income payments (SSI), reaching out to
those eligible for SSI payments, improving social
security coverage for women based on the
couple's earned income, reforming private pension
plans, eliminating ageism in employment, and
improving economic opportunity through
employment.

11-18.   Older Women: The Economics of Aging.
         Women's Studies Program and Policy
         Center at George Washington University,
         1980.

Women comprise the majority of those 65
and older. Most older women are widows
although most older men are married and living
with their wives; older women are more likely to
live alone than older men. Older women have

considerably lower incomes than older men, with
black women having the lowest median income.
Also, women are dependent solely on social
security to a greater extent than are men, yet
women receive lower benefits.

11-19. On the Other Side of Easy Street: Myths and Facts
about the Economics of Old Age.
Washington, DC: Villers Foundation,
1987.

Though poverty among the elderly is less
widespread than it once was, it still exists. This
report attempts to disprove several myths about
the economic well-being of the elderly by pointing
out that poverty is severe among several
subgroups, including women and minorities, who
are not well protected by safety-net programs.

11-20. Porcino, Jane. "The Feminization of Poverty for
Midlife and Older Women and Its Effects
on Their Health." 1985. (ERIC
microfiche ED264505)

Poverty prevents many aging women from
securing good health care. The 41 percent of
women over 65 who live alone are the poorest of
the poor, with an annual income for white women
of $3000 and for black, $2000. This abject poverty
prevents access to good medical care, and there is
a lack of community- and home-based health care
and preventive health services. There is a need
for specially trained workers for the aging, for
long-term insurance protection, and for more
research into osteoporosis, breast cancer, and
hormone therapy.

11-21. Rodeheaver, Dean, and Nancy Datan. "The Challenge of Double Jeopardy: Toward a Mental Health Agenda for Aging Women." <u>American Psychologist</u> 43 (1988): 648-654.

　　　　While the aged are at risk due to the increased problems they face as part of growing older, women are doubly at risk because they also face problems of gender, especially poverty, widowhood, and the dynamics of family caregiving. One of the most significant effects of poverty is seen in widowhood where inactivity, isolation, poor health, and diminished financial resources predict psychological risk and argue for the advisability of mental-health services.

11-22. Rosenblatt, Jean. "Women and Aging." <u>Editorial Research Reports</u>, September 25, 1981, pp. 715-732.

　　　　The problems of aging are to a great extent the problems of women. The reality of older women's lives includes loneliness, failing health, poverty, and widowhood. Living alone, unemployment, inadequate health care, and inequities in the social security system and pensions contribute to older women's slide into poverty. Remedies include legislation and changes in society's negative stereotyping of older women.

11-23. Scott, Jean Pearson, and Vira R. Kivett. "The Widowed, Black, Older Adult in the Rural South: Implications for Policy." <u>Family Relations</u> 29 (1980): 83-90.

　　　　Following the White House Conferences on Aging in 1961 and 1971, Congress amended the Social Security Act and the Older Americans Act to better serve the elderly. However, the needs of the rural elderly, especially the black elderly, are not met by local delivery of services. This population needs an income floor, health, housing, and transportation services.

11-24. Smith, Ken R., and Phyllis Moen. "Passage Through Life." Sociological Quarterly 29 (1988): 503-524.

As women move into mid-life, they typically witness their last child leaving home and the dissolution of their marriages due to divorce or widowhood. This significantly alters their economic well-being and affects their employment patterns.

11-25. Snyder, Eloise. Women, Work and Age, Policy Challenges: Proceedings of a Conference. Ann Arbor, MI: Institute of Gerontology, University of Michigan, 1984.

The results of a conference dedicated to the issue of work and older women (defined here as those over 40). Participants considered issues such as age discrimination, federal programs such as Aid to Families with Dependent Children (AFDC) and the Omnibus Budget Reconciliation Act (OBRA) of 1981, union organizing, black women, pensions and social security, fringe benefits, job training, occupational safety and health, and part-time work. Each section includes recommendations for change and a bibliography.

11-26. "The Status of Older Women in Illinois Today: A Report by the Task Force on Older Women in Illinois." Illinois State Department on Aging. 1986. (ERIC microfiche ED279922)

Older women make up 60 percent of the elderly over 65 in Illinois. Public hearings have revealed that older women are more at risk because of their limited incomes, poor housing, and inadequate health care. Women are living longer and are more likely to live alone and in poverty. The feminization of poverty nationwide reflects the experience of older women in Illinois. Older women receive half the retirement income of older men. Older women need increased benefits, jobs, expanded pension laws, housing options, long-term health care, and expanded protective services.

11-27. Stone, Robyn I. "The Feminization of Poverty Among the Elderly." Women's Studies Quarterly 17 (1989): 20-34.

Elderly women have a much higher poverty rate than elderly men. The feminization of poverty among older Americans is due to gender inequities in the social security system and in private pension plans; the sexual division of labor, which assigns primary family responsibilities to women; labor market discrimination which results in lower earnings during working life, lower pension benefits, and less employment at older ages; and impoverishment if their husbands are institutionalized.

11-28. U.S. Congress. House. Select Committee on
Aging. Quality of Life for Older Women:
Older Women Living Alone. 100th
Congress, 2nd Session. Washington, DC:
Government Printing Office, 1989.
(Y 4.Ag 4/2:L 62/3)

This hearing was held to examine options
for improving the quality of life for older women.
Witnesses, including social scientists and
representatives of advocacy groups like the Older
Women's League and the National Organization
for Women, were asked to address the quality of
life of older women, their needs, and how federal
policies could be adapted to help them. They
discussed issues such as social security and health
care.

11-29. U.S. Congress. House. Select Committee on
Aging. The Quality of Life for Older
Women Living Alone. 100th Congress,
2nd Session. Committee Print.
Washington, DC: Government Printing
Office, 1989. (Y 4.Ag 4/2:L 62/2)

The summary report of the Committee's
hearing (see #11-28 above). The circumstances
and needs of elderly women are different from
those of elderly men, although policymakers and
researchers often use the experience of men as
the norm. More than three-quarters of the
elderly living alone are women. Older women are
disproportionately the victims of poverty, partly
because of their limited participation in the labor
force, low wages, and discrimination. Their health
care needs are different from men's. This
publication summarizes testimony of witnesses on
income, health, and housing, and includes a
discussion of issues and policy recommendations
for each.

11-30. U.S. Congress. Joint Economic Committee. The
Role of Older Women in the Work
Force. 98th Congress, 2nd Session.
Washington, DC: Government Printing
Office, 1984. (Y 4. Ec7: W84/9).

Older women in the work force still
encounter ageism and sexism, and, in the case of
women of color, racism. This hearing examines
these and other problems of older women
workers, such as the lack of skills, experience, and
education. Witnesses describe labor-force
participation and inadequate income of older
women.

11-31. U.S. Government Accounting Office. An Aging
Society: Meeting the Needs of the
Elderly While Responding to Rising
Federal Costs. 1986. (ERIC microfiche
ED276949)

The General Accounting Office (GAO)
reports on the failure of retirement income to
provide for the cost of acute health care and long-
term care services for the elderly. While the
retirement income status of the elderly has
improved, several groups are still poor, including
women, minorities, and persons age 85 and over.

11-32. Van Sickle, Carol. "Jobless at 61: A Success Story."
Ms., October 1986, pp. 66-68.

After 13 years of service and at the age of
61, Van Sickle's corporation abolished her job in a
cost-cutting effort. She recognized this as an ego-
shattering experience, analyzed her skills, and
repackaged herself for a part-time job with the
same company.

11-33. Warlick, Jennifer L. "Aged Women in Poverty: A
        Problem Without a Solution?" In Aging
        and Public Policy: The Politics of
        Growing Old in America, pp. 35-66.
        Edited by William P. Brown and Laura
        K. Olson. Westport, CT: Greenwood
        Press, 1983.

        Warlick paints a bleak picture of the
economic status of aged women. She presents
statistical evidence to document and explain the
higher incidence of poverty among aged females
than among aged males. The reasons include
sporadic work histories, the high percentage of
women who work in jobs not covered by private
pensions, and benefit computation rules for social
security and other government transfers that favor
married couples. Despite women's increased
labor-force participation, their average job status
or eligibility for private pensions has not
increased. Comprehensive social security reform
is unlikely because of concerns about the system's
financial soundness. Policies designed explicitly to
address the needs of aged women will be required
to bring about any improvements in the economic
status of aged women.

11-34. Warlick, Jennifer L. "Why is Poverty After 65 a
        Woman's Problem?" Journal of
        Gerontology 40 (1985): 751-757.

        Poverty continues to be a women's
problem. Women are likely to be widowed and to
have had an interrupted work history at sex-
segregated low-paying jobs due because of both
childrearing responsibilities and discrimination in
the marketplace.

11-35. Wisensale, Steven K. "Generational Equity and Intergenerational Policies." <u>Gerontologist</u> 28 (1988): 773-778.

There seems to be an emerging and organized backlash against the social interests of the aged, and the elderly lobby may be required to advance its agenda through state rather than federal legislation. At the state level, the elderly will be forced to share agendas with families, youth and children, and to develop intergenerational packages. After Reagan, a reduction in the military budget and increase in taxes may reduce the deficit and diffuse the clash between generations.

11-36. Wisniewski, Wendy, and Donna Cohen. "Older Women: A Population at Risk for Mental Health Problems." 1984. (ERIC microfiche ED258073)

The aged are the fastest-growing subgroup of the American population, and it is increasingly peopled by the extreme aged. With advancing age, older women are more likely to confront poverty, widowhood, living alone, institutionalization, and chronic multiple illness including the risk of mental-health problems. The highest incidence of alcoholism in women occurs in widows, and women are more frequent users of psychotropic drugs. The rates of clinical depression are higher for women than for men and may be explained by social discrimination and other sexist inequities.

11-37. Wood, Vivian. "Older Women and Education." 1981. (ERIC microfiche ED199576)

Education has the potential to change the economic and social picture for middle-aged women. Education is correlated to a woman's

earning power and, as in the instance of
widowhood, a woman's social integration.
Returning women students need an educational
tax deduction, tax credit, or entitlements not
unlike the GI Bill.

12   Social Security, Pensions, and Retirement

The social security system is one of the largest and oldest public programs in the history of the United States. It was designed in the thirties to help working Americans live out their lives in dignity and decency. However, as the years have passed, it has become clear that the social security system works better for some people, mostly men, than for others, mostly women. The social security program assumes that men are breadwinners and that women are dependents, a relationship that is no longer the pattern for most of the population, as more women work outside the home and as the divorce rate increases. Even women who fit the stereotype of dependent homemaker are penalized by the system.

Under the social security system, a woman who is not married to the same man for ten years has no protection. A widow receives no benefits until age 60, unless she cares for dependent children. She will receive full benefits only if she waits until age 65 to retire. If a homemaker reaches retirement age with her husband, her benefits will be equal to only half of his. Should the spouse retire early, and thus receive reduced benefits, the homemaker's benefits will also be reduced. If, at any time after retirement, the husband decides to return to work, the wife's benefits will also be terminated.

The married woman who works outside the home is penalized in other ways. The working wife is entitled to collect benefits based on either her own wage record or her husband's, whichever is higher. The woman who earns less than her husband must pay into a system from which she will never collect as an individual, but only as a dependent of her spouse.

Women who work are penalized by the system when they leave their jobs to have children. Currently, social security benefits are based on average lifetime earnings with only the five lowest years dropped out of consideration. Therefore, every additional year that a woman spends out of the paid labor force caring for children becomes, for the purposes of averaging her income, a year in which she earned zero.

Women also suffer under pension plans because they tend to work at lower-wage jobs which either have no pension plans or pay so little that pension benefits are minimal. Furthermore, since many women move in and out of the labor market while raising families, they may never work long enough at one job to vest in a pension. Also, divorce may result in loss of a husband's pension benefits, with no recompense for years of unpaid labor in the home.

Proposals for reform of social security include earnings-sharing plans, which are based on the principle that each spouse is an equal partner in marriage and that each makes an economic contribution to the marriage, whether inside or outside the home. The couple's total earnings would be divided equally between them for the years they were married for the purpose of computing retirement benefits. Other plans would give homemakers credit for the years they spend working in the home.

12-1. Abramowitz, Mimi. "The Family Ethic and the
Female Pauper: A New Perspective on
Public Aid and Social Security Programs."
Journal of Social Work Education 21
(1985): 15-26.

Applying a gender-lens to social welfare
policy, Abramowitz finds that the welfare state is
shaped by the family ethic. Women are
encouraged to find a male breadwinner or to
accept a low standard of living. Aid to Families
with Dependent Children encourages women to
stay home and become dependent on the state,
while the social security benefit structure assumes
a woman's economic dependence on a man.
Welfare state programs will serve all families
properly when they no longer make traditional
assumptions about women's roles.

12-2. Anthony, Sandra. "Social Security: The Unkindest
Cut of All." Union W.A.G.E., no. 66,
July/August 1981, pp. 3-4.

Health and Human Services Secretary
Schweiker makes protestations about the
inescapable crisis of social security benefit cuts
which mask reality. Social security is not a system
that goes broke. By proposing to reduce
retirement benefits for people aged 62 to 64 and
forcing people to work until age 65, the Reagan
Administration hoped to save $17.6 billion
between 1982 and 1986. Few workers have this
choice: they retire early because they are sick or
laid off or because they choose to do something
else with their lives. The new policy hurts the
many women and blacks who retire early.
Professionals, not domestics and coal miners, want
to remain in the labor force.

12-3. Bell, Donald, and Avy Graham. "Surviving Spouse's Benefits in Private Pension Plans." Monthly Labor Review 107 (April 1984): 23-31.

The law requires private pension plans to offer a lifetime minimum annuity to surviving spouses of about two-fifths of a worker's accrued benefits. However, both eligibility requirements for this benefit and the size of monthly payments depend on when death occurs. The article reports on data from a 1981 Bureau of Labor Statistics survey of employee benefits in large and medium-sized firms. Although all private pension plans include some provision for survivors' benefits, the surviving spouse can lose these benefits if the active worker dies prior to eligibility for the spouse's benefits, if a survivor-benefits plan was not selected (at additional cost) before retirement or the couple does not meet the one-year marriage requirement, or if the joint-and-survivor annuity was waived by the employee at retirement.

12-4. Bennett, Carol T. F. "The Social Security Benefit Structure: Equity Considerations of the Family as Its Basis." American Economic Review 69 (1979): 227-231.

The present system of social security payments based on family type (single, married, divorced) produces inequities as the benefits are financed through payroll taxes. The insurance premiums of larger families are subsidized by the contributions of smaller families, regardless of ability to pay. This is true despite the strong weighting of the system in favor of lower-income workers. Bennett suggests that in order to rectify this inequity among families and individuals, social security benefits should no longer be allocated on the basis of family pattern. Instead, she proposes to have social security benefits and contributions added to the income tax system. Low-income families would receive a tax credit against payroll taxes and pay no taxes on benefits received, while benefits received by higher-income families would be taxed at the family's marginal tax rate.

12-5. Brilmayer, Lea, and others. "Sex Discrimination in Employer Sponsored Insurance Plans: A Legal and Demographic Analysis." University of Chicago Law Review 47 (1980): 505-560.

In 1972, the Supreme Court rejected a retirement plan which statistically associated sex and mortality and allowed different payouts to men and women (City of Los Angeles v. Manhart, 435 U.S. 702, 1978). In Los Angeles, women had been making greater contributions than men but receiving the same benefits. Sex-segregated actuarial tables attribute the entire difference in mortality to sex alone, not to self-destructive behavior men engage in. Should men change their behavior and enjoy good health, they will enjoy greater benefits. Women do not have this option, as their benefits are fixed at the lower female level. There is little evidence that women enjoy universal, biological health advantages over men. Gender is a spurious, weak, and unstable predictor of mortality.

12-6. Burkhauser, Richard V. "Are Women Treated Fairly in Today's Social Security System?" Gerontologist 19 (1979): 242-249.

Two-earner households are now in the majority, and the Old Age Survivors Insurance model of the one-earner family is obsolete. The social security system must be adjusted to provide for more equitable survivor benefits.

12-7. Burkhauser, Richard V., and Karen C. Holden, eds.
<u>A Challenge to Social Security: The
Changing Roles of Women and Men in
American Society</u>. New York: Academic
Press, 1982.

This volume includes papers from a
conference sponsored by the Institute for
Research on Poverty. The authors examine
options for changing the treatment of men and
women by social security programs. Options
include homemaker credits, a community-property
notion of family earnings, a double-decker plan,
and a two-tier plan. The authors discuss the
assumptions about women's work behavior
inherent in each plan.

12-8. Burnett, Barbara A. "Family Economic Integrity
Under the Social Security System."
<u>NYU Review of Law and Social Change</u>
7 (1978): 155-186.

The social security program created in
1935 provides benefits for the majority of the
workforce upon retirement, as income
replacement. However, complete retirement
security cannot be provided under Social Security,
and it would be more realistic to promote the
economic stability of the family based on the
economic interdependence of family members.
The contribution of the non-income-earning
spouse should be counted toward social security
benefits; families with two wage earners should
receive the same credits as families with one wage
earner earning the same total income. The social
security system should not infringe upon individual
arrangements and freedom of personal choice in
matters of income earning, child care, or family
income. The benefits of social security should
have an equal impact on all families. For this to
happen, the benefit structure must be sex-neutral,

thereby allowing for maximum flexibility within the family structure.

12-9. Card, Emily. "Retirement Security: A Mix-and-Match Approach." Ms., June 1986, pp. 66-69.

Before the inflation of the seventies and the deficits of the eighties, people built their retirement security on social security benefits, home ownership, and a portfolio of other resources. But today many people aged 45 and under cannot bank on home ownership, and their social security retirement benefits may be inadequate.

12-10. Forman, Maxine. "Social Security is a Women's Issue." Social Policy 14 (1983): 35-38.

Despite the government's official position on how well the elderly are doing, most of the elderly have their options limited by race or gender, especially blacks, Hispanics, people with income under $10,000, and women. Women make up 60 percent of the elderly and 60 percent of those living on social security benefits. As workers, spouses, and survivors, women's benefits are very low, due to their low wages in a discriminatory marketplace, time out of the workforce for homemaking, and provisions treating divorced women and elderly widows inadequately.

12-11. Froomkin, Daniel. " 'Easy Vote' on Insurance Gender Gap Turns Out to be a Tough Political Call." National Journal 15 (July 13, 1983): 1545-1549.

The insurance industry is strenuously resisting the pressure from women's and civil rights groups to eliminate gender differences in rates and benefits. Relying on statistics that show different longevity, sickness, and accident rates for women and men, insurance companies charge different rates for life, health, and auto insurance, and for retirement annuities. Advocates for change argue that legislative correction would advance economic equity for women, while opponents claim that it would hurt the consumer. The Supreme Court has ruled against inequities in retirement benefits, and most employer-related pension plans are now gender-neutral. Individually purchased life annuities remain the exception. The National Organization for Women estimates that sex discrimination in insurance costs the average woman $15,372 over her lifetime.

12-12. Judah, Ann. "Pensions, Social Security Inadequate; Women Get Hit the Hardest." Union W.A.G.E, no. 62, November/December 1980, p 1+.

Social security simply does not pay enough. Women receive less than men, and single women less than married women. Suggestions for reform include income-averaging between married couples, sharing of earnings records at divorce, inheritance of earnings credit upon death of spouse, and allowing more than five dropout years. Small steps toward equality would not be enough to bridge the gap in retirement pay between women and men until women achieve equal pay while working.

12-13. Kahne, Hilda. "Women and Social Security: Social
Policy Adjusts to Social Change."
International Journal of Aging and
Human Development 13 (1981): 195-208.

   The social security system needs reform,
as women live longer and outlive men. Because
of their domestic roles and limited rewards of
their paid employment, their retirement income is
inadequate. Immediate reforms in the system
should allow the surviving spouse to inherit
earnings credit for the years married, splitting of
earnings credit for divorced couples for a
marriage that has lasted a minimum of ten years,
adjustments in survivor benefits to account for
increases in productivity and standard of living,
and evaluation of the status of groups of women
who remain below the poverty line despite the
reforms.

12-14. Kaltenborn, Sara H. "Social Security: A Proposal
to Improve Equity and Adequacy for
Women." Journal of Legislation 8 (1981):
250-262.

   Whereas social security has grown to be
the largest public income-maintenance program in
the country, it is essential that it have a cost-of-
living index and provide equitable treatment for
women. Kaltenborn proposes earnings sharing, a
method of splitting earnings credit between wife
and husband for the years of marriage, reflecting
the philosophy that marriage is an economic
partnership, and that assets accumulated during
marriage, including social security earnings, should
be shared equally, regardless of how the couple
chose to allocate homemaking and paid-work
responsibilities.

12-15. Lopata, Helena Znaniecka, and Henry P. Brehm. <u>Widows and Dependent Wives: From Social Problem to Federal Program</u>. New York: Praeger, 1986.

Lopata and Brehm examine social security and the economic situation of American women and find that the focus of the program is on men. They trace the history of the economic dependency of women and children in America, beginning in colonial times, through the Social Security Act of 1935, and the 1939 changes in the law, as well as more recent changes. Another section of the book consists of a study of Chicago-area widows. The authors also studied a thousand women between the ages of 24 and 54 to determine whether women are now less dependent on men in their adult years, and to examine their knowledge of and attitude toward social security. They conclude by reviewing recent attempts to reform the system.

12-16. Quadagno, Jill. "Women's Access to Pensions and the Structure of Eligibility Rules: Systems of Production and Reproduction." <u>Sociological Quarterly</u> 29 (1988): 541-558.

While some feminists argue that women's lower pension rates are due to interruptions in work histories, Quadagno argues that they are due to the failure of pension rules to recognize women's reproductive labor. She finds the workplace to be the institution most pervaded by male domination, and pensions, which are a product of union-employer negotiations, to reflect the gender inequality in the work-place. She calls for full equality between social production and reproduction, and greater sensitivity to women's patterns of labor-force participation.

12-17. Rogers, Gayle Thompson. "Aged Widows and OASDI Mothers' Benefits (impact of a proposal that would terminate mother's and father's benefits when the youngest child in the care of a surviving spouse reaches age 16, rather than age 18, as in current law)." Social Security Bulletin 44 (February 1981): 3-18.

This study reports on the decisions of widows to apply for benefits under Old-Age, Survivors, and Disability Insurance (OASDI) of the Social Security Act. Eligibility usually begins at age 60, and because of financial need, most widows elect benefits at the earliest possible time. Those who were working and well-off at the time of widowhood tended to postpone receiving their benefits. Most widows experienced a reduction in their standard of living.

12-18. Sass, Tim. "Demographic and Economic Characteristics of Nonbeneficiary Widows: An Overview." Social Security Bulletin 42 (November 1979): 3-14.

A survey of widows under age 60 and without dependent children (and thus ineligible for monthly social security benefits) found that their income was low, about $6,144 a year. Earnings were by far the most important source of income, much more important than their husbands' pension benefits.

12-19. U.S. Congress. House. Select Committee on
Aging. Inequities Toward Women in the
Social Security System. 98th Congress,
1st Session. Washington, DC:
Government Printing Office, 1983.
(Y 4.Ag 4/2:In 3)

Women's low retirement benefits reflect
both their low wages as workers and inequities in
the social security system. Furthermore, working
spouses can usually expect to receive a benefit
that is less than if they had never worked or paid
into the system at all. This hearing includes
testimony from a variety of experts on proposals
to redress inequities.

12-20. U.S. Congress. House. Select Committee on
Aging. Women's Pension Equity. 98th
Congress, 1st Session. Washington, DC:
Government Printing Office, 1983.
(Y 4.Ag 4/2:W 84/9)

This hearing includes testimony from
representatives of women's groups, lawyers,
actuaries, and accountants on methods and
consequences of sex equity in public and private
pension plans. In 1983, 60 percent of single
women over age 65 depended entirely on social
security, yet a woman's average benefit was only
$4,476, compared to a man's average $5,724.

12-21. "Women and Social Security." Social Security
Bulletin 48 (February 1985): 17-26.

A survey conducted by the Social Security
Administration showed an increase in average
benefits and in pension receipt rates for both
women and men. Of women entering retirement
in 1982, the majority were married, and they and
their husbands received social security benefits
above the poverty level and also received

pensions. Unmarried women received benefits above the poverty threshold; unmarried female retired workers were as likely as unmarried men to receive pensions in addition to social security benefits. Survivor benefits from husbands' pensions were more likely to be available to women than in the past.

13   Teenage Mothers and
Their Children

The United States has the highest teenage pregnancy rate in the industrialized world. Over the past 20 years a national decline in fertility levels has characterized a broad range of social groups within the United States, including women at all socioeconomic levels, racial and ethnic backgrounds, and religious groups.

In contrast, the number of pregnancies and births among unmarried adolescent girls has greatly increased. In 1970, there were about 2 million births to teenage mothers; by 1986 that number rose to 2.9 million. (Statistical Abstract of the United States 1989, Washington, DC: Government Printing Office, 1989, Table 93.) In addition, more girls are choosing to keep their babies rather than give them up for adoption, and fewer teenagers are marrying the fathers of their babies. According to Andrew Hacker, 99.3 percent of black girls and 92.6 percent of white girls who give birth decide to keep their babies. (Andrew Hacker, "American Apartheid," New York Review of Books, December 3, 1987, p. 27.)

In a report released by the School of Social Service Administration at the University of Chicago, Professor Mark Testa, one of four authors, has challenged the conservative view presented by Charles Murray in Losing Ground: American Social Policy 1950-1980 (Basic, 1984). Testa claims that male unemployment leads to female single-parenting. According to the Chicago study, employed males are willing to marry the mothers of their children. Murray claims that employed men do not marry because the couple would risk losing the woman's welfare payments.

The Chicago study showed different rates for marriage in the inner-city: for example, among fathers who conceived their first child before marriage, only 29 percent of the blacks and 27 percent of the Puerto Ricans married the mother of the child within three years. By contrast, 62 percent of the Mexican-Americans surveyed and 74 percent of non-Hispanic whites eventually married the women. (William Schmidt, "Study Links Male Unemployment and Single Mothers in Chicago," New York Times, January 15, 1989, p. 16, col. 5.)

Teenage pregnancy is perhaps the most critical issue facing the black community. Although white teenage pregnancy has increased dramatically, it lags behind the number of black teenage pregnancies. Pregnant white teenagers are not as poor as their black counterparts. They come from varied socioeconomic backgrounds and are more likely to have an abortion or to place the child up for adoption. Generally, should a white teenager choose to keep her child, she receives greater economic assistance from her family than does the typical black teenager.

The black teenage mother usually has a child in her mid-teens, comes from a family that subsists on an income below the poverty level, and is unmarried at the time her child is born, though she may marry before she reaches adulthood. Over 80 percent of the births to black teenagers occur outside of marriage and some 90 percent keep their children rather than place them in adoptive homes. (Joyce A. Ladner and Ruby Morton Gourdine, "Intergenerational Teenage Motherhood: Some Preliminary Findings," Sage 1 [1984]: 22-24.)

The most significant consequence of teenage parenthood has been the increase in the poverty of young mothers without resources and training who are unable to move out of poverty into an increasingly highly trained labor force. Adolescent pregnancy and parenthood are clearly linked to poverty and long-term welfare dependency. (U.S. Congressional Budget Office, <u>Reducing Poverty Among Children</u>, Washington, DC: CBO, 1985, p. 108.) Teenage mothers are more likely to drop out of school and to have more children than their peers who delay motherhood. They therefore have reduced labor force participation and earnings, and a disproportionate number of AFDC (Aid to Families with Dependent Children) recipients are or were teenage mothers.

Teenage pregnancy and childbearing are now viewed as significant problems over the long term with negative psychological, social, medical, educational and economic impact. Pregnant adolescents have been found to be obstetrically at risk, with mortality rates highest among teen mothers and their babies. (U.S. Congressional Budget Office, <u>Reducing Poverty Among Children</u>, Washington, DC: CBO, 1985.) Experts, such as the staff of the Alan Guttmacher Institute, have proposed solutions ranging from prevention programs, including health clinics in high schools, to comprehensive services such as education, job training, and child care, for those girls who get pregnant and keep their babies.

13-1. Adler, Emily Stier, Mildred Bates, and Joan M. Merdlinger. "Educational Policies and Programs for Parents and Pregnant Teenagers." Family Relations 34 (1985): 183-187.

Education is found to be a significant factor in young women's labor-force participation after an early pregnancy. Though there were 1.1 million teenage pregnancies reported in 1978, 80 percent of which were unintended, there are no national educational policies to deal with the prevention of teenage pregnancy or its outcomes. More and more, this policy formation will be the responsibility of local governments.

13-2. Baldwin, Wendy, and Virginia S. Cain. "The Children of Teenage Parents." Family Planning Perspectives 12 (February 1980): 34-43.

Teenage childbearing is associated with adverse, pervasive, and long-lasting social and economic consequences for adolescent mothers, who are also at higher risk for maternal mortality. Given their lower education and income and greater marital instability, it might be expected that their children would also be adversely affected. There is some evidence that good prenatal care can produce a healthy infant, but infants, especially males, suffer developmentally from the social and economic consequences of early childbearing.

13-3. Burden, Dianne S., and Lorraine V. Klerman. "Teenage Parenthood: Factors That Lessen Economic Dependence." Social Work 29 (1984): 11-16.

The incidence of teenage pregnancy is directly related to the increase in female-headed single parent families. In 1979, the out-of-wedlock birthrate for black teenagers was seven times that for whites. Teen-parenting is a major cause of the feminization of poverty, and teenage mothers have high rates of welfare dependence. Teen-parenting is the logical outcome of the sex role socialization of women in America, especially black teenagers, who are devoid of meaningful career opportunities. These mothers need to complete their education and receive job training and experience in order to alleviate their poverty.

13-4. Cartoof, Virginia. "The Negative Effects of AFDC Policies on Teenage Mothers." Child Welfare 61 (1982): 269-278.

Federal and state welfare policies are not committed to improving the quality of family life. In the absence of a national family policy, the ideology of individualism and the horror of creeping socialism subvert government proposals. The task is to redesign the Aid to Families with Dependent Children system to promote an individual's efforts to get off welfare. Teenage mothers should not have to be separated from their families in order to receive welfare, and there should be child-care subsidies. Welfare departments' attempts to enforce child-support payments from fathers are humiliating and further disrupt young mothers' support networks.

13-5. Chilman, Catherine S. "Teenage Pregnancy: A Research Review." Social Work 24 (1979): 492-498.

Chilman reviews current social and psychological research about the apparent causes and consequences of teenage pregnancy. Although the number of births, not the rate of births to adolescents, rose in the sixties and early seventies, the growing phenomenon is that 90 percent of unmarried teenage mothers choose to keep their babies. The causes of teenage single-parenting include the changing norms about sex, the influence of racism, poverty, low levels of educational achievement and aspirations, as well as limited communication between parents and children. The deleterious health consequences for mother and baby are related more to poverty and poor nutrition than to youth. It is unlikely that teenagers become pregnant to get public assistance. Social service programs should not target only the pregnant teenager but provide comprehensive services for all family members.

13-6.   deAnda, Diane. "Pregnancy in Early and Late Adolescence." Journal of Youth and Adolescence 12 (1982): 33-42.

Comparing early and late teenage pregnancy, deAnda found that fewer younger teenagers used birth control measures, though both groups used them only sporadically. Young (12-17) teens began dating and going steady earlier than older (18-20) teens. She urges more education about sexuality, reproduction, and birth control within the context of interpersonal relations.

13-7.   Dillard, K. Denise, and Louis G. Pol. "The Individual Economic Costs of Teenage Childbearing." Family Relations 31 (1980): 249-260.

There is growing recognition of the high costs of early childbearing and large families because they reduce the educational achievement and average annual income of women. The hidden costs of children born to teenagers make these children proportionately more expensive than others. Women who bear their first children as teens face a lifetime of economic stress and limited opportunities. Disproportionately represented among AFDC mothers are women with little schooling, female household heads, women with limited work experience, and teenage mothers.

13-8. Franklin, Donna L. "Race, Class and Adolescent Pregnancy: An Ecological Analysis." American Journal of Orthopsychiatry 58 (1988): 339-354.

Using an ecological development model, Franklin analyzes the high rate of adolescent pregnancy in the United States, especially among low-income blacks. The multiple determinants of this problem include factors operating on the individual, family, sociocultural, and social-structural levels. Earlier sexual activity among blacks, intergenerational single-parenting, the culture of poverty, and lenient public welfare policies encourage unmarried black women to have children. Intervention must be directed at all levels if birthrates are to be lowered.

13-9. Furstenburg, Frank F., Jr. "Burdens and Benefits: The Impact of Early Childbearing on the Family." Journal of Social Issues 36 (1980): 64-87.

In studying teenagers in Baltimore and Philadelphia, residential patterns provided a useful way of indicating family support. By moving out of the parental household, the teenaged mother reduced the subsidies provided by her family, e.g., room and board, and lessened the chances that a relative would be available to provide child care. Most teenage mothers stayed close to home, and the adolescent's family shouldered much more responsibility when she remained single than when she married. All but a few parents lent assistance to their daughters. Daughters were much more likely to remain in couple-headed households than in female-headed households, and they were more likely to continue their schooling as parental families became involved in childrearing responsibilities.

13-10. Furstenberg, Frank, Jr., and others. "Adolescent Mothers and Their Children in Later Life." Family Planning Perspectives 19 (1987): 142-51.

The authors dispute the popular belief that early childbearing almost certainly leads to dropping out of school, subsequent unwanted births, and economic dependence. A significant minority of the young mothers who participated in the study gave birth in the sixties and saw their lot as having improved. They have continued their schooling, found employment, become independent of welfare, established their own households, and limited their childbearing. However, the majority did not fare as well as they would have had they postponed parenthood.

13-11. Furstenburg, Frank F., Jr., Richard Lincoln, and Jane Menken, eds. Teenage Sexuality, Pregnancy and Childbearing. Philadelphia: University of Pennsylvania Press, 1981.

A collection of articles that originally appeared in Family Planning Perspectives between 1972 and 1980. Among them are "The Health and Social Consequences of Teenage Childbearing," "The Social Consequences of Teenage Parenthood," "Economic Consequences of Teenage Childbearing," "The Children of Teenage Parents," and "Adolescent Pregnancy Prevention Services in High School Clinics."

13-12. Gilchrist, Lewayne D., and Steven Paul Schinke.
"Teenage Pregnancy and Public Policy."
Social Service Review 57 (1983): 307-322.

The annual cost to the federal
government in medical and welfare expenditures
for the 460,000 teenage pregnancies is more than
$8.3 billion. The economic costs of early
parenthood are supported by welfare, as half of all
payments go to women who first bore children in
adolescence. In the seventies, abortion was
legalized and contraception became more
accessible, and both became free of parental
monitoring. Future social policy should improve
pregnancy prevention through school health
education and services, though such programs are
opposed by conservatives. The government will
need to bridge the gap between parents and
children in the transmission of sexual values and
in the monitoring of adolescents' sexual behavior.

13-13. Gispert, Maria, and others. "Predictors of Repeat
Pregnancies Among Low-Income
Adolescents." Hospital & Community
Psychiatry 35 (1984): 719-723.

Using a client group of teenage girls who
had been pregnant once during a two-year period
and comparing them to a group of girls who had
become pregnant at least twice during the same
period, the author found that the predictors of
repeat pregnancies included the use of
contraception, the quality of the relationship
between the girl and her mother, and the presence
of the girl's father in the home. Pregnancy-
prevention programs for groups similar to those
studied here (low-income, black, semi-rural
families with many children) should not neglect
parental involvement. The researchers agree with
some of the recent political moves to ensure that
parents are notified of their daughter's request for
contraception.

13-14. Grow, Lucille, J. "Today's Unmarried Mothers;
The Choices Have Changed." <u>Child
Welfare</u> 58 (1979): 363-372.

By the mid-seventies single mothers
began to shift from giving their children up for
adoption to keeping their children. Women who
opt for adoption are now in the minority and
reflect the traditional values of previous decades,
that children need two-parent homes.

13-15. Hansen, Holger, George Stroh, and Kenneth
Whitaker. "School Achievement: Risk
Factor in Teenage Pregnancies."
<u>American Journal of Public Health</u> 68
(1978): 753-759.

In upstate New York, these three doctors
looked at educational achievement prior to
teenage pregnancies. As expected, teenagers
doing poorly in school had a high incidence of
pregnancy. Unexpectedly, so did young teenagers
who were ahead of their peers scholastically. The
relation of school achievement and pregnancy risk
varied according to age and race.

13-16. Hofferth, Sandra L., and Kristin A. Moore. "Early
Childbearing and Later Economic Well-
Being." <u>American Sociological Review</u> 44
(1979): 784-815.

There is surprisingly little empirical
evidence for the widely held belief that earlier
childbearing has numerous social and economic
consequences, such as lowered educational
achievement, larger families, lower earnings, and
poverty. The authors' evidence indicates,
however, that age of first birth does affect
education and earnings, less so for black women
than for white. Later childbearers (those who
delay until age 27) are economically better off

because total family size is reduced; their total work experience and earnings are greater, as are those of husbands and other family members.

13-17. Hogan, Dennis P., and Evelyn M. Kitagawa. "The Impact of Social Status, Family Structure and Neighborhood on the Fertility of Black Adolescents." American Journal of Sociology 90 (1985): 825-855.

   The authors take an ethnographic look at young (ages 13-19) black women in the Chicago ghetto, investigating whether economic uncertainties postpone marriage, while many young women achieve adulthood through premarital parenthood. Socialization in a female-headed family or in a family where sisters have become teenage parents enhances the acceptability of early intercourse and parenthood. Against the loosely defined and enforced norms of sexual behavior, parents are powerless to regulate successfully their childrens' behavior.

13-18. Hollingsworth, D. R., and A. K. Kreutner. "Teenage Pregnancy." New England Journal of Medicine 303 (1980): 516-518.

   Today, one in five births in America is to a woman 18 years of age or younger. Births to older teenagers have decreased, but births to mothers 15 to 17 years old have increased. Teenage pregnancy is common to all social, economic, and racial groups in all parts of the nation. Teenage pregnancies have unique medical, social, behavioral, and emotional consequences which warrant its prevention, as well as the availability of prenatal care and access to first-trimester abortion.

13-19. Ladner, Joyce A. "Black Teenage Pregnancy: A Challenge for Educators." Special Issue: The Black Child's Home Environment and Student Achievement. <u>Journal of Negro Education</u> 56 (1987): 53-63.

There is a multiplicity of factors causing adolescent pregnancy among blacks, not least of which are the restriction of educational and training opportunities and poverty. Traditionally the black community was more tolerant of out-of-wedlock births, neither labeling the mother as deviant nor the child as illegitimate nor forcing the surrender of the child for adoption. The most serious problem resulting from early parenting is the lack of educational advancement and resulting unemployment. Ladner advocates family-planning education, life-skills training, sex education, and school-based health clinics.

13-20. Ladner, Joyce A., and Ruby M. Gourdine. "Intergenerational Teenage Motherhood: Some Preliminary Findings." <u>Sage</u> 1 (1984): 22-24.

The crisis in black families is due to the phenomenon that 50 percent of households are female-headed and consequently poor. Their poverty is linked to a variety of health and social problems. Teenage pregnancy is, perhaps, the most crucial issue facing the black community. Over 80 percent of the births occur outside of marriage, and 90 percent of teenagers elect to keep their children rather than place them for adoption. Increased urbanization and a relaxation of societal attitudes help to explain the soaring rate of teenage childbearing. There is a quiet resignation to this plight, so resources are stretched further in intergenerational households causing greater stress and bleaker prospects.

13-21. Lincoln, Richard. "Is Pregnancy Good for
        Teenagers?" USA Today 107 (July
        1978):34-37.

        Two-thirds of the teenagers who become
pregnant do not want the pregnancy, and about
one third have abortions. Teenage mothers suffer
economically with lower educational attainment
and health complications as a result of pregnancy.
Their marriages tend to be less stable. Teenagers
need realistic sex education, along with adequate
health insurance, counseling services for
contraception and abortion, and adequate prenatal
care.

13-22. McKenry, Patrick C., Linda H. Walters, and
        Carolyn Johnson. "Adolescent Pregnancy:
        A Review of the Literature." Family
        Coordinator 28 (1979): 17-28.

        The authors criticize the literature on
adolescent pregnancy as tending toward
description and advocacy and lacking sophisticated
methodology for studying broader populations and
theoretical models concerning the etiology of
adolescent pregnancy and the behavior of
pregnant adolescents.

13-23. Moore, Kristin A. "Teenage Childbirth and
        Welfare Dependency." Family Planning
        Perspectives 10 (1978): 233-237.

        This article summarizes the results of a
study by the Center for Population Research of
the National Institute of Child Health and Human
Development commissioned by Congress to
estimate the cost of teenage childbearing to the
government through Aid to Families with
Dependent Children (AFDC). In 1975, the
federal government disbursed $9.4 billion to
households through AFDC, about half to

households containing women who had borne
their first child while still teenagers. Teenage
childbearing interrupts schooling, limits
employment opportunities, and often leads to
welfare dependency. Moore identifies several
points for intervention, including programs aimed
at assisting young mothers in staying in school and
equal employment opportunities. The study
refutes the belief that AFDC provides economic
incentives for early births.

13-24.   Moore, Kristin A., and others. <u>Teenage
          Motherhood: Social and Economic
          Consequences</u>. Washington, DC: Urban
          Institute, 1979.

The overall decline in the fertility rate
and the disproportionate increase in childbearing
among females under the age of 17 is a cause for
concern. This report indicates that teenage
childbearing leads to important negative
consequences for the young mother and her
family and triggers a chain of events that combine
to undermine later social and economic well-
being. Education, family size, marriage and
marital instability, participation in the labor force
and earnings, welfare dependency, and poverty are
all affected by early childbearing. The data
persuaded researchers that the postponement of
first birth would have improved the life of the
teenage mother. All in all, early childbearers
seem to experience more difficulties and endure
more unhappiness and end up less well-off than
women who postpone childbearing. Their
children's lives are also affected as they
experience greater economic and emotional
deprivation, more poverty and welfare
dependency.

13-25. National Research Council. Panel on Adolescent
Pregnancy and Childbearing. Risking the
Future: Adolescent Sexuality, Pregnancy,
and Childbearing. 2 vols. Washington,
DC: National Academy Press, 1987.

The panel investigated the causes and
consequences of teenage pregnancy and
recommended possible solutions. Volume I
includes the panel's findings, conclusions, and
recommendations. Volume II contains reviews of
research and statistical data on which Volume I is
based.

13-26. Ortiz, Elizabeth Thompson, and Betty Bassoff.
"Adolescent Welfare Mothers: Lost
Optimism and Lowered Expectations."
Social Casework 68 (1987): 400-405.

Early pregnancy and parenthood are
established indicators of high-risk status for both
mother and child with regard to future health
problems, poverty, child abuse, and neglect, and
the exceptionally high rate of teenage pregnancy
in the U.S. contributes substantially to its social
and economic problems. This social work study
describes the views of a sample of teenage welfare
mothers about important life issues such as
career, education, motherhood, sexuality, and
projections about the future. The study found the
young welfare mothers to be consistently less
optimistic about the future than their nonparent
peers. Their experience of early parenthood
significantly altered their perceptions of reality
and caused them to lower their life expectations.

13-27. Peabody, Elle, Patrick McKenry, and Leandro
          Cordero. "Subsequent Pregnancy Among
          Adolescent Mothers." Adolescence 16
          (1981): 563-568.

          The medical and social problems
associated with teenage pregnancy are further
complicated by subsequent pregnancies.
Programs designed to encourage adolescents to
postpone additional pregnancies must extend
beyond the first year after delivery, make
contraceptive information accessible, and
encourage contraceptive use.

13-28. Perlman, Sylvia B., Lorraine V. Klerman, and E.
          Milling Kinard. "The Use of Socio-
          Economic Data to Predict Teenage Birth
          Rates. An Exploratory Study in
          Massachusetts." Public Health Reports
          96 (1981): 335-341.

          Teenage birthrates vary by geographic
area and are associated with certain
socioeconomic factors. Despite the availability of
contraceptives and abortion in Massachusetts,
poverty tended to be causally linked to high
fertility rates among teenagers. In communities
with low median incomes, with a high proportion
of families on welfare, and with high fertility rates
in the previous generation, teenagers will bear
children at a higher rates than in communities
with the opposite characteristics.

13-29. Polit, Denise F., and Janet R. Kahn. "Early
          Subsequent Pregnancy Among
          Economically Disadvantaged Teenage
          Mothers." American Journal of Public
          Health 76 (1986): 167-171.

          Data gathered over a two-year period
from a sample of 675 teenage mothers living in

eight American cities showed that more than half
of the sample population became pregnant again.
The high incidence of teenage pregnancy in the
U.S., higher than in any other industrialized
country, has a range of negative consequences,
including infants at risk, high rates of divorce,
educational deficits, and economic hardship for
the mother. Minority teenagers are most at risk
as they are most likely to suffer economic
consequences. Early repeat pregnancies were
found to occur at a fairly high rate among
adolescent mothers. The authors were stymied by
their inability to predict which teenagers would
experience a repeat pregnancy.

13-30. Stiffman, Arlene, and others. "Adolescent Social
Activity and Pregnancy:
Socioenvironmental Problems, Physical
Health and Mental Health." Journal of
Youth and Adolescence 16 (1987): 497-
509.

The association between adolescent
pregnancy, socioenvironmental forces, and physical
and mental health problems are examined in this
paper. The authors found that early sexual
activity and pregnancy are associated with
psychosocially disadvantaged backgrounds.
Nonetheless, despite their disadvantaged
backgrounds, pregnant teenagers do not suffer
greater physical and mental-health deficits than
their nonpregnant peers who are sexually active,
although sexually inactive youths have the lowest
rate of mental health problems. Therefore,
education and birth control information alone will
not reduce the rate of teenage pregnancy without
effective psychosocial intervention in unstable
families.

13-31. Teenage Pregnancy in Industrialized Countries.
New Haven, CT: Yale University Press,
1986.

The project reported here was carried out
by the Alan Guttmacher Institute to study the
relatively high adolescent birthrates and abortion
rates in the U.S., compared to Canada, England
and Wales, France, the Netherlands, and Sweden.
The purpose of the comparison was to understand
the determinants of teenage pregnancy in the U.S.
and those factors that might be subject to policy
changes. Although American adolescent sexual
activity is on par with that of other countries,
white teenage pregnancy rates are higher, and
black rates higher still. Clearly, it is possible to
achieve a lower pregnancy rate. Several proposed
innovations include school-based health clinics
that provide contraceptive services, enhancement
of the current family-planning clinic system,
increased health coverage through health
maintenance organizations, sex education courses
in public schools, availability of information about
sexuality and contraception through the media.
These approaches are tempered by America's
heterogeneous population, conservative religious
groups, government ambivalence about providing
wide-ranging social and welfare benefits, income
inequities, and well-funded constituencies that
oppose contraception, sex education, and legalized
abortion.

13-33. Tietze, Christopher. "Teenage Pregnancies:
Looking Ahead to 1984." Family
Planning Perspectives 10 (1978): 205-208.

About 1.1 million teenagers are dealing
with pregnancies, few of them intended. If legal
barriers such as parental notification or consent
laws reduce teenagers' access to contraception, or
if the proportion of sexually active teenagers
increases, or if more adolescents initiate sexual

activity at younger ages, teenage pregnancies will be likely to increase.

13-34. U.S. Congress. House. Committee on Post Office and Civil Service and Committee on Energy and Commerce. <u>Demographics of Adolescent Pregnancy in the United States</u>. 99th Congress, 1st Session. Washington, DC: Government Printing Office, 1985. (Y 4.P 84/10:99-5)

Includes statistics from the Census Bureau, the Department of Health and Human Services, and the Alan Guttmacher Institute on the incidence of teenage pregnancy in the U.S. Also includes testimony on the economic and health consequences of teenage pregnancy for mothers and their children, as well as policy options for preventing teenage pregnancy and for assisting teenagers after they become pregnant.

14 Health, Nutrition, and Hunger

Over the years, national surveys have provided evidence of the relationship between poverty and health. In the United States, access to health care is generally dependent on ability to pay. As a consequence, poor women are dependent upon government-funded social welfare programs to attain access to health care. Furthermore, poor families and single parents suffer a level of family stress higher than any other demographic group. Poor women suffer from the physical and mental consequences of poverty, the life- and property-threatening events consistent with living in poor neighborhoods, and early parenthood.

The Medicaid program, enacted in 1965 by an amendment to the Social Security Act, provides a broad range of health-care benefits to poor, eligible individuals. Medicaid has greatly increased the amount of health care that poor people receive. Yet, despite substantial annual investments in health care for the poor, problems remain. A significant portion of poor individuals are not eligible for the program; those who are enrolled are more likely than the non-Medicaid population to receive fragmented and episodic care in high-cost settings; and steady, preventive health care is still far from the norm. Low levels of Medicaid reimbursement make private physicians reluctant to treat Medicaid patients, and the poor must often go to crowded public clinics for care.

The United States has one of the highest rates of infant mortality among industrialized nations, and the infant mortality rate for blacks is nearly twice that for whites. Low birth weight (5.5. pounds or less) is the major cause of infant mortality, and it can lead to lifelong physical and mental problems for those babies who survive. Early intervention and prenatal care can reduce the risk. However, the very women who need prenatal care the most are the least likely to get it.

Reproductive health represents a critical area of health care for poor and minority women because it includes those aspects of health currently subject to public legislation. Abortion, sterilization, and contraception are issues important to all women, but because poor and minority women are dependent on public funding for reproductive health services, their personal health needs are infringed upon by public policy and practice. In July 1989, the Supreme Court decision in Webster v. Reproductive Health Services, while not explicitly overturning the Roe v. Wade decision legalizing abortion, greatly increased the power of the states to restrict abortion. Restriction of access to abortion services affects poor women who cannot afford to pay for an abortion or to travel to a state where abortions are easier to obtain.

One rapidly escalating public health problem which has disproportionately affected poor and minority women and children is the incidence of AIDS. Equally devastating to poor families is the growing use of crack cocaine in the inner cities. Compared to heroin, crack addicts more quickly and its use is more prevalent among women. The growing addiction of poor ghetto women strikes at the strongest linchpin of ghetto families and neighborhoods -- mothers. Babies born to crack users are often born addicted. They suffer behavioral and developmental problems, and, in the case of "boarder babies", are left in the hospital by their mothers. Increasingly, grandparents, usually grandmothers, have to assume responsibility for their children's children. ("Crack's Hidden Toll: The Destruction of Families," New York Times, June 23, 1988, p. A1, col. 5.)

14-1. Amaro, Hortensia. "Considerations for Prevention of HIV Infection Among Hispanic Women." Psychology of Women Quarterly 12 (1988): 429-443.

Data on the characteristics of individuals diagnosed with AIDS shows that Hispanic women, men, and children are overrepresented. Although Hispanics represent only 7 percent of the general population, they represent 15 percent of all AIDS cases. AIDS prevention programs must be designed in light of the characteristics of Hispanic women, their lower educational achievement, early pregnancies, lower earnings, lack of reproductive information, and linguistic and cultural separation. The lack of success of traditional health-care delivery models among Hispanics indicates the need for innovative programs involving community-based organizations.

14-2. Arendell, Teresa. "Unmarried Women in a Patriarchal Society: Impoverishment and Access to Health Care Across the Life-Cycle." In Poverty and Social Welfare in the United States, pp. 53-81. Edited by Donald Tomaskovic-Devey. Boulder, CO: Westview, 1988.

In a patriarchal capitalist society, women are subordinated to men both in the family and in the labor market. Arendell examines the health consequences of being a poor single woman in such a society for women in three categories: single mothers with dependent children, mid-life displaced homemakers, and aged women. She outlines the health problems of each group and discusses the inadequacies of programs like Medicare, Medicaid, and Social Security.

14-3. Bennett, Maisha B. H. "Afro-American Women, Poverty and Mental Health: A Social Essay." Women and Health 12 (1987): 213-228.

There is a strong link between poverty and mental health. Mental illness experienced by poor black women results from inadequate resolution of poverty-induced stresses. These women experience unemployment or underemployment, sickness and disability, female headship, and racism. For them marriage is not a realistic option, and they struggle with motherhood and poverty, household responsibilities, and intergenerational welfare dependency. They can become submerged in the culture of poverty. They need extensive mental health programs geared toward changing attitudes and behaviors that perpetuate poverty. This approach needs to be coupled with educational and employment opportunities.

14-4. Chirikos, Thomas N., and Gilbert Nestel. "Further Evidence on the Economic Effects of Poor Health." Review of Economics and Statistics 67 (1985): 61-69.

Sex and race comparisons of the economic effects of poor health show the impact of poor health to be greater than anticipated and to exact a different toll from each race. Blacks are less able than whites to sustain employment and income when sick. Since blacks have a higher prevalence of health problems, health problems account for a sizable proportion of the wage gap between the black and white populations. White women are better able than men or black women to sustain ill health through work reassignment or job mobility. White women also engage in more compensatory work activity while their health is improving. However, women and blacks are less likely to receive vocational rehabilitation services.

14-5. Colletta, Nancy D. "At Risk for Depression: A Study of Young Mothers." Journal of Genetic Psychology 142 (1983): 301-310.

Colletta found high rates of depression among single mothers, especially those with young children. Adolescent mothers suffer the additional stresses of interrupted or terminated education, high unemployment rates, low-level occupations, and poverty. However, when young mothers were involved in supportive social networks, levels of depression decreased.

14-6. Couto, Richard A. "Fair Starts for Children: An Assessment of Rural Poverty and Maternal and Infant Health Care." 1985. (ERIC microfiche ED275480)

Couto investigated improving prenatal and infant care as a means of reducing infant mortality and low-birthweight babies. These problems are often associated with the poverty of their parents, especially their mothers. One means to improve and deliver needed care is a home visitor program which serves women who are at high risk for problem pregnancies. Sampling a mixed population, Couto found that age and race determined the amount of information women had about health matters. Younger and poorer women had less access to transportation and limited support systems. Women in female-headed households who were unemployed reported more unplanned pregnancies and less preventive child health care. Couto points out the need for more resources for low-income women and their children and for a community-based home visitor program.

14-7. Cummings, Michele, and Scott Cummings. "Family Planning Among the Urban Poor: Sexual Politics and Social Policy." Family Relations 32 (1983): 47-58.

The Cummingses look at one of the most enduring controversies in family social welfare: how poor and minority women plan their families. There is widespread opinion that the poor should limit the size of their families to enhance their life options and to move away from intergenerational poverty. Family planning intervention strategies should consider the culture and history of client groups when developing birth-control programs.

14-8. "Faces of Hunger in the Shadow of Plenty." Senate Interim Committee on Hunger and Nutrition. 1984. (ERIC microfiche ED263230)

Hunger is a growing problem in Texas, affecting the elderly, women and children, and the "new poor" hard hit by the recent recession. The legislature wants to appropriate $12 million worth of supplemental funds, develop statewide nutritional education, referral and monitoring programs, streamline and disseminate food stamp programs, agricultural donations and community gardens, and increase AFDC payments.

14-9. Fisher, Elliot S., and others. "Prenatal Care and Pregnancy Outcomes During the Recession: The Washington State Experience." American Journal of Public Health 75 (1985): 866-869.

This study examines the adverse impact of the economic recession of 1981-1982 on poor pregnant women in Washington State as unemployment increased and Medicaid eligibility decreased. More women residents of low-income areas received delayed prenatal care or none at all, and they delivered, proportionately, more low-birthweight babies.

14-10. Friedman, Samuel R., and others. "The AIDS Epidemic Among Blacks and Hispanics." Milbank Quarterly 65 (1987): 455-499.

A disproportionate number of people with AIDS are black and Hispanic. There have been few studies of race and AIDS, resulting in a lack of funding and programming designed to assist the minority community. Minorities know more about issues that depend on knowledge carried by street grapevines than by professional promulgation.

14-11. Garland, Barbara K. "The Possible Effects of Nutritional Status and Growth of Children on the Economic Potential of West Virginia." 1985. (ERIC microfiche ED275483)

Nutritional policy affects the productivity of the population, shown by Japan's postwar nutritional policy which increased the size and performance of its population. West Virginia suffers from the highest rate of postneonatal deaths and physically immature children in the nation, along with high unemployment rates. There is evidence that entitled female heads of households are not participating in food-assistance programs such as Food Stamps or WIC (Women, Infant and Children Supplemental Food Program).

14-12. Gladow, Nancy W., and Margaret P. Ray. "The Impact of Informal Support Systems on the Well-Being of Low Income Single Parents." Special Issue: The Single Parent Family. Family Relations 35 (1986): 113-123.

The results of the authors' study indicate that informal networks of friends and relatives affect the four measures of well-being used: loneliness, isolation, happiness, and total problems. These networks, more than church and community supports and the presence of a lover, indicate that forming friendships may enhance well-being among low-income single parents more than do love relationships. Social service agencies should encourage the development of skills in forming relationships.

14-13. Henshaw, Stanley K., and Lynn S. Wallisch. "The Medicaid Cutoff and Abortion Services for the Poor." Family Planning Perspectives 16 (1984): 170-180.

Following the legalization of abortion in 1973, poor women paid for their abortions through Medicaid coverage. In 1976, the Hyde Amendment severely limited Medicaid-funded abortions. Since 1981, Medicaid abortions have been funded only when the woman's life is in danger should she carry the pregnancy to term. Studies have shown that women who were formerly eligible for Medicaid-funded abortions sought them instead from nonphysicians or had self-induced abortions. Often abortions were postponed to the second trimester and paid for at the expense of food and clothing for their children.

14-14. Herold, Joan, and Ingrid Waldron. "Part-Time
Employment and Women's Health."
Journal of Occupational Medicine 27
(1985): 405-412.

There is a relationship between
employment and self-reported physical health,
where full-time employed women report the best
health, part-time workers, intermediate levels of
health, and women who are out of the labor force,
the poorest health. These relationships, however,
are affected by race and marital status. Married
black women and unmarried women who worked
part-time reported worse health than full-time
workers. In this national sample of middle-aged
women, married white women reported little
health differences whether they were part- or full-
time workers. The low socioeconomic status of
black women may explain their poorer health.
Poor health, in turn, may motivate black wives to
seek part-time employment.

14-15. Kenney, Asta M., and others. "The Medicaid
Expenditures for Maternity and Newborn
Care in America." Family Planning
Perspectives 18 (1986): 103-110.

A national survey by the Alan
Guttmacher Institute found that Medicaid
subsidized 15 percent of all women who gave
birth. Because of inadequate reimbursement,
many doctors and hospitals are reluctant to take
Medicaid patients. The authors argue that
bringing Medicaid payments into line with
marketplace charges would improve health
outcomes for low-income women and their babies.

14-16.   Lang, Dorothy T. "Poor Women and Health
                 Care." Clearinghouse Review 11 (1981):
                 1056-1060.

          Access to health care in America is
determined by income, race, and sex; poor people
have less access than affluent. Poor women suffer
as men control the delivery of health services and
determine the quality of health care women
receive.

14-17.   McBarnette, Lorna. "Women and Poverty: The
                 Effects on Reproductive Status." Women
                 and Health 12 (1987): 55-81.

          Since access to health care in the United
States depends upon ability to pay, the poor are at
risk and are dependent on government-funded
social welfare programs. Poverty is a health
problem, as is teenage childbearing. The poor
lack family planning services, are susceptible to
sexually transmitted diseases resulting in ectopic
pregnancies and AIDS babies, and are at greater
risk for maternal deaths and cervical cancer. The
authors call for enforcement of the right to health
care as part of a new social contract between
women and the state.

14-18.   Nsiah-Jefferson, Laurie. "Reproductive Laws,
                 Women of Color, and Low-Income
                 Women." Women's Rights Law Reporter
                 11 (1989): 15-38.

          Women of color and poor women have
fewer choices in reproductive health care than do
other women. Two overriding concerns are the
availability of new technology and safeguarding
against abuse. The author discusses six areas of
reproductive health: time limits on abortion,
prenatal screening, the fetus as patient,
reproductive health hazards in the workplace,

interference with reproductive choice, and
alternative means of reproduction. Each section
ends with a set of policy recommendations.

14-19. Rathbone-McCuan, Eloise. "Health Needs and
Social Policy." Women and Health 10
(1985): 17-27.

Rathbone-McCuan describes
demographic and economic factors that impinge
on the health care of elderly women, as well as
policies that control access to and utilization of
health and long-term care services. She notes
some of the shortcomings of past policies and
recommends social reform efforts aimed at
greater policy equity for older women.

14-20. Reissman, Catherine Kohler. "The Use of Health
Services by the Poor: Are There Any
Promising Models?" Social Policy 14
(1984): 30-40.

Despite improvements since the sixties,
social class and race continue to limit access to
health care. Cuts in health programs which serve
the poor have resulted in avoidance of
overcrowded and inconveniently located clinics
and hospitals. Although services have been
curtailed, doctors fight for alternative services
such as childbirth centers and pediatric home
care. Research shows that it is not the culture of
poverty, but rather structural inequities in the
health-care system that limit access to health care.

14-21. Richardson, Hilda. "The Health Plight of Rural
Women." Women and Health 12 (1987):
41-54.

Poor women have difficulty obtaining
needed health services due to their poorer health

status and lesser ability to pay for services. Rural poor women are also isolated from resources commonly available in urban areas, such as public transportation and the availability of a wide range of health resources. Strategies to address the health plight of rural women must address their poverty and include a coherent national and state rural health policy that recognizes rural health as a distinct part of the health-care system.

14-22. Springer, Philip B. "Health Care Coverage of Survivor Families with Children: Determinants and Consequences." Social Security Bulletin 47 (February 1984): 3-16.

When a male breadwinner dies, his young family loses his earnings as well as such fringe benefits as group health insurance, which are not replaced by Social Security payments. (Group health insurance is cheaper than private insurance, and its coverage is greater.) This makes widows and their young children especially vulnerable as they can afford less medical care, have higher expenditures for health care, and in general are in poorer health than the population at large.

14-23. Tallon, James R., and Rachel Block. "Changing Patterns of Health Insurance Coverage: Special Concerns for Women." Women and Health 12 (1987): 119-136.

Women, especially poor women, are vulnerable to gaps in health insurance coverage and are denied access to health care. Medicaid restrictions deny health care to many female heads of households because of income and other eligibility restrictions. The authors argue for universal health insurance. In the meantime, the poor can benefit from the expansion of Medicaid, insurance, and direct payments to providers of health-care services.

14-24. Texidor del Portillo, Carlotta. "Poverty, Self-Concept and Health: Experience of Latinas." Women and Health 12 (1987): 229-242.

Soon to be America's largest minority group, Hispanics are on the lowest rung of the economic ladder, suffering from poor health and poor self-concept. Based on her 20 years of counseling Hispanic women at the San Francisco Mission Community College Center, Texidor del Portillo urges short-term counseling for clients who have low self-esteem and wish to change their economic status.

14-25. U.S. Congress. House. Committee on Energy and Commerce. Infant Mortality Rates: Failure to Close the Gap. 98th Congress, 2nd Session. Washington, DC: Government Printing Office, 1984. (Y 4.En 2/3:98-131)

In 1984, the mortality rate of black infants was approximately twice that of whites. In this hearing, health experts and social scientists discuss the reasons for the high rate: poverty, unemployment, lack of health insurance, inadequate prenatal care, inadequate nutrition, and substance abuse. Despite the undeniable need for prenatal care, the Reagan Administration budget cuts reduced the availability of such care for poor women.

14-26. U.S. Congress. House. Select Committee on Children, Youth, and Families. <u>Born Hooked: Confronting the Impact of Perinatal Substance Abuse</u>. 101st Congress, 1st Session. Washington, DC: Government Printing Office, 1989. (Y 4.C 43/2:P 41)

Testimony of doctors, nurses, and public health officials on the effects of crack cocaine on pregnant women and their babies. Issues include the impact on the health-care and foster-care systems, behavioral and developmental problems of the children, the increasing numbers of grandparents who have assumed responsibility for their grandchildren, need for increased availability of treatment, and the problem of boarder babies.

14-27. U.S. Congress. House. Select Committee on Children, Youth, and Families. <u>Continuing Jeopardy: Children and AIDS</u>. 100th Congress, 2nd Session. Washington, DC: Government Printing Office, 1988. (Y 4.C 43/2:Ac 7/4)

An update to <u>Generation in Jeopardy: Children and AIDS</u> (See #14-28). Includes statistics on the growth in the reported number of pediatric AIDS cases. Many infants, known as boarder babies, spend much of their lives in the hospital. The committee noted that the federal response, both in terms of funding and policy leadership, is still too little.

14-28. U.S. Congress. House. Select Committee on
Children, Youth, and Families.
Generation in Jeopardy: Children and
AIDS. 100th Congress, 1st Session.
Washington, DC: Government Printing
Office, 1988. (Y 4.C 43/2:Ac 7/3)

Results of a study undertaken by the
Select Committee. Includes chapters on the
dramatic increase in AIDS among infants and
young children, the disproportionate effect of
AIDS on minority children, the escalating costs of
caring for children with AIDS, AIDS and
adolescents, prevention strategies, and the lack of
federal resources devoted to AIDS prevention and
treatment for children and youth. Updated by
Continuing Jeopardy: Children and AIDS (see
#14-27).

14-29. U.S. Congress. House. Select Committee on
Narcotics Abuse and Control. Cocaine
Babies. 100th Congress, 1st Session.
Washington, DC: Government Printing
Office, 1988. (Y 4.N 16:100-1-16)

Increasing numbers of children are being
born to mothers who used cocaine during
pregnancy. Many are born prematurely. Some
suffer withdrawal symptoms. Most suffer long-
term effects. Often their mothers have received
little or no prenatal care. The Committee's
hearing includes information on the extent of the
problem, implications for the children, and policy
options, such as increased access to drug
rehabilitation and improved prenatal care.

14-30. U.S. Congress. House. Select Committee on
Narcotics Abuse and Control. <u>Pediatric
AIDS Hearing</u>. 100th Congress, 1st
Session. Washington, DC: Government
Printing Office, 1988. (Y 4.N 16:100-1-
10)

Pediatric AIDS cases are primarily a
result of IV drug use by the child's mother or her
partner. The incidence is disproportionately high
among black and Hispanic children who may live
in an environment of poverty and drug abuse.
Poor children and their families lack access to
support service and health care. Witnesses at this
hearing discussed the extent of the epidemic, the
difficulty of affecting changes in behavior that
would prevent transmission of the virus, and
health and educational needs of children with
AIDS.

14-31. United States Conference of Mayors. "The Status
of Hunger in Cities." Task Force on
Joblessness and Hunger. 1985. (ERIC
microfiche ED269496)

In its survey of hunger in American cities
after the recession of 1981-1982, the U.S.
Conference of Mayors found that, even though
the economy recovered, the hunger problem grew
by 35 percent and is expected to increase even
more. Congress must be sensitive to this problem
as it considers reauthorization of the food stamp
program, surplus commodity distribution and
other domestic food-assistance programs. The
Conference urges the expansion of all federal
food-assistance programs.

14-32. Zambrana, Ruth E. "A Research Agenda on Issues Affecting Poor and Minority Women: A Model for Understanding Their Health Needs." Women and Health 12 (1987): 137-160.

Low-income women face multiple barriers as they attempt to secure health care for themselves and for their families under socioeconomic conditions which promote mental and physical illness. Their health status has to be understood in terms of race, class, and gender. Ethnic minority women experience higher infant mortality rates, prevalence of diabetes, hypertension, cardiovascular disease, cervical cancer, teenage pregnancies, and lower life expectancy.

15   Housing and Homelessness

In <u>Rachel and Her Children: Homeless Families in America</u>, (Crown, 1988), Jonathan Kozol describes various methods of estimating the number of homeless in America and concludes, "We would be wise ... to avoid the numbers game. Any search for the 'right number' carries the assumption that we may at last arrive at an acceptable number. There is no acceptable number." (p. 10) Whatever number of homeless Americans there are now, it is clear that their numbers have increased in the last few years. The composition of the homeless population has also changed: from the stereotypical single male alcoholic to increasing numbers of the deinstitutionalized mentally ill and families.

Families are homeless because they cannot find affordable housing. In many cities, gentrification has reduced the stock of affordable rental housing. Furthermore, the Reagan Administration virtually eliminated federal funds for the construction and rehabilitation of low-income housing.

Women lacking housing and decent jobs and wages take to the streets as social services fail to meet their needs. Because of their sex-role socialization, women's dependency makes them fare less well on the street then men. Rape is prevalent and the lack of privacy seems to be more critical for women than for men; it is often the reason given for refusing to enter public shelters. (Stephanie Golden, "Sheltering Women: The Forgotten Homeless," <u>City Limits</u>, January 1988, pp. 12-16.) Homeless children who grow up in shelters and welfare hotels are exposed to the drug culture, prostitution, intermittent schooling and lack of health care and social services, including school breakfast and lunch programs.

Housing activists have called upon the federal government to fund an income-based housing entitlement assistance program to enable low-income people to obtain decent housing at costs they can afford; to provide an adequate and affordable housing along with the preservation, construction and rehabilitation of existing housing stock without displacing people; to encourage resident control and strengthen and enforce fair housing laws and equal opportunity requirements; and to reform tax laws and provide funding to encourage low-income and moderate-income housing.

15-1.   Anderson, Sandra C., Tom Boe, and Sharon Smith. "Homeless Women." Affilia 3 (1988): 62-70.

       In the study population, 190 homeless women in Portland, Oregon, living in shelters with their dependent children, the authors found histories of physical or sexual abuse, poor health, institutionalization, and alcoholism. Because of their low incomes they were unable to find affordable housing. They also need dependable child care, job training, and public assistance. They were not happy eccentrics who enjoyed living on the streets.

15-2.   Bachrach, Leona L. "Homeless Women: A Context for Health-Planning." Milbank Quarterly 65 (1987): 371-396.

       The literature fails to recognize the gender differences in the homeless population and the special circumstances of homeless women. They seem to be more invisible than men. Life on the streets can be an adaptation to poverty, a choice of the least restrictive environment for the disaffected. Bachrach discusses the health needs of homeless women, who need comprehensive intervention allowing continuity of care.

15-3.   Bassuk, Ellen L. "The Feminization of Homelessness: Families in Boston Shelters." American Journal of Social Psychiatry 7 (1987): 19-26.

       Homeless families compose the fastest-growing subgroup of homeless persons. Homelessness is due to inadequate housing supply, low welfare benefits, and the breakdown in family structure. This study of homeless families in the Boston area finds the typical family to be female-headed, young, and with dependent

children. It is not only the economics of poverty
that create homelessness but a "tangle of
pathology". Dr. Bassuk recommends an
emergency program in the shelters and a national
policy of affordable housing to rescue families,
and especially children, from a lifetime of
deprivation and violence.

15-4. Galowitz, Paula. "Poor Women and Housing."
Clearinghouse Review 11 (1981): 1060-
1064.

Although obtaining decent housing is the
top priority of all people, women-headed
households suffer systematic discrimination in
securing and maintaining adequate housing. The
Fair Housing Act (Civil Rights Act of 1986)
forbids discrimination in housing based on sex but
does not protect women against exclusion as
welfare mothers from government subsidized
housing. However, it does provide the legal
framework to pursue the housing rights of welfare
mothers.

15-5. Hagen, Jan L. "Gender and Homelessness." Social
Work 32 (1987): 312-316.

Women and men experience
homelessness differently. The traditional image of
the homeless person has been that of an older,
white male alcoholic living on skid row. During
the seventies, the homeless population increasingly
began to include younger men and women of all
ages. Minorities were over-represented.
Vulnerability to physical abuse places women and
girls at increased risk for homelessness. Men are
more likely to experience homelessness due to
unemployment, alcohol abuse, and jail release.

15-6. Hagen, Jan L., and Andre M. Ivanoff. "Homeless Women: A High-Risk Population." Affilia 3 (1988): 19-33.

Nationwide, families constitute more than 20 percent of the homeless population, and this number is expected to triple as affordable housing becomes even more scarce. In this study of homeless women in Albany, New York, the most important reason given for homelessness was family problems, followed by unemployment, which left families unable to pay the rent or to meet mortgage payments. The authors urge emergency shelters and food for the homeless, along with mental health services, and, most importantly, safe affordable housing.

15-7. Kozol, Jonathan. Rachel and Her Children: Homeless Families in America. New York: Crown, 1988.

Kozol describes the lives of homeless families, many of them headed by women, in New York City's welfare hotels. He delves into the circumstances that led to their becoming homeless and describes life in the hotels.

15-8. Newman, Sandra J., and Ann B. Schnare. Subsidizing Shelter: The Relationship Between Welfare and Housing Assistance. Urban Institute Report 1. Washington, DC: Urban Institute Press, 1988.

The authors point out that housing has been, for the most part, left out of the welfare reform debate. They argue that cutbacks in federal housing programs during the Reagan Administration have reduced the number of affordable housing units. They believe that the two-stream approach--housing and welfare--leads to inefficiency, inequity, and ineffectiveness.

15-9. Roberts, Ron E., and Thomas Keefe. "Homelessness: Residual, Institutional and Communal Solutions." <u>Journal of Sociology and Social Welfare</u> 13 (1986): 400-417.

Although President Reagan said that the homeless are homeless by choice, the authors find that the homeless population consists of the unemployed, alcoholics, the mentally ill, and recently evicted, elderly, and single mothers who have been separated or divorced and are unable to meet mortgage payments or rent. The homeless in America are symptomatic of the decay of the social and economic system as it lurches from boom to bust. They require, as do other social casualties, a fundamental restructuring in social services.

15-10. Roth, Dee, Beverly G. Toomey, and Richard J. First. "Homeless Women: Characteristics and Needs." <u>Affilia</u> 2 (1987): 6-19.

A statewide survey of homeless women in Ohio found that the causes of homelessness are economic and family problems. The women studied were young and predominately white. Programs must provide safe shelters and rehabilitation plans connecting women to income maintenance programs, mental health care, and training in social and vocational skills. It is helpful to view the problems of homeless women as extremes of the normal lack of social, emotional, and economic resources for women.

15-11. Stoner, Madeleine R. "The Plight of Homeless Women." <u>Social Service Review</u> 57 (1983): 565-581.

Describing the homeless population and the special needs of women who are homeless,

Stoner points out that a population once
dominated by older alcoholic white men now
includes more women, elderly, and young people.
The antecedents of homelessness are lack of
housing, unemployment and poverty,
deinstitutionalization, and domestic violence and
abuse. Homeless women do not choose to live on
the streets; they are victims of forces over which
they have no control. There needs to be a
comprehensive housing and service system for the
homeless.

15-12. Vermund, Sten H., and others. "Homelessness in
New York City: The Youngest Victims."
New York State Journal of Medicine 87
(1987): 3-5.

Homelessness is increasing among
American families due to the increase in the
proportion of families falling below the poverty
line and to the shortage of low-cost housing.
Pregnant women who are homeless are
significantly less likely to receive adequate
prenatal care, are more likely to have low-
birthweight babies, and to have a child die in the
first year of life than women of similar
socioeconomic status in New York City housing
projects. Homelessness is a significant factor in
infant mortality, prenatal care, and low
birthweight.

15-13. U.S. Congress. House. Select Committee on
Children, Youth, and Families. The
Crisis in Homelessness: Effects on
Children and Families. 100th Congress,
1st Session. Washington, DC:
Government Printing Office, 1987.
(Y 4.C 43/2:H 75)

This hearing includes the testimony of
activists, social scientists, and homeless parents

and children on the causes and consequences of homelessness. Families are homeless because they are poor, and they enter shelters only after they have exhausted the support of family and friends. The effects of homelessness on children include developmental delays, emotional problems, and health problems. Furthermore, they are often unable to attend school. Solutions to the problem includes increased availability of low-income housing and a shelter system that would keep families intact.

15-14. Wright, James D., and Julie A. Lam. "Homelessness and the Low-Income Housing Supply." Social Policy 17 (1987): 48-53.

The traditional homeless population-- hoboes and skid-row bums--is now supplemented by the new homeless, who are younger, better-educated, and more likely to be members of racial and ethnic minority groups. This increasing homelessness is due to a virtual decimation of the low-income housing supply in most large American cities. Homelessness is a housing problem. Not only has the average price of rental housing increased, many low-income units have either been destroyed or converted to more profitable uses. The authors contend that regardless of the pathologies found among the homeless and the provision of well-intended social services, the availability of affordable housing is the solution to the problem of homelessness.

16   Welfare Issues

The issue of public assistance to families who are unable to provide a minimal level of subsistence through the largest of such programs, Aid to Families with Dependent Children (AFDC), provokes passion and hostility. Conservatives argue that there are few truly needy among the welfare population and that the solution to the real needs of other families is employment. Charles Murray believes that attempts to reduce poverty actually made things worse, since poverty increased as federal social spending increased. George Gilder argues that welfare has undermined the family by offering more than a male wage earner can provide. Liberals argue that although there are families on welfare who should probably not be, welfare is required as a safety net to insulate the poor from the fluctuations in the economy.

Public assistance was established in the thirties along with Social Security for widows and children. Today with the revolution in the status of the family and the transition to the female-headed family, AFDC is the only financial alternative available to women, mostly with children, who are unable to support themselves with earnings and child support. The financial support for AFDC families is substantially below every measure developed of what is an adequate subsistence level, although there are proponents of myths to the contrary. The mayor of New York City, Edward I. Koch, writing in the New York Times (4 March 1988, p. A39, col. 2) lends his voice to those who speak of the soft life enjoyed by generations of family members on the dole. He writes about the welfare mother who refused 19 apartments before she found the right one and the welfare father who has sired 19 children. Despite such hostile views, AFDC remains a minimal, short-term program.

The average AFDC family has three members, and most families remain on AFDC less than two years. Well over half of the AFDC recipients have children under the age of six; more than 10 percent of AFDC recipients are unable to work because of illness or a handicapping condition. The greatest numbers of AFDC families are single-parent, female-headed households who are unable to provide economically for their children. Their participation in public assistance and other public transfer programs such as food stamps and housing allowances maintains their income at below the estimated poverty level.

Concern about rising welfare costs and behavioral dependency, the belief that welfare recipients ought to work for their money, and a growing consensus on parents' obligations to support their children led in the mid-eighties to efforts to reform the welfare system, culminating in the 1988 Family Support Act. See Chapter 17 (Welfare Reform and Workfare) for further discussion of welfare reform.

16-1. Au Claire, Philip A. "The Mix of Work and
            Welfare Among Long-term Welfare
            Recipients." Social Service Review 53
            (1979): 586-605.

        Research indicates that even among long-
term AFDC (Aid to Families with Dependent
Children) recipients, earnings constitute a
significant portion of total family income. The
more educated client will mix work and welfare
but will not necessarily leave the welfare rolls.
This is due to the dual labor market and the low
wages of women and minorities and implies that
complete economic independence cannot be the
only goal pursued by welfare policy.

16-2. Bahr, Stephen J. "The Effects of Welfare on
            Marital Stability and Remarriage."
            Journal of Marriage and the Family 41
            (1979): 553-560.

        This study found that low-income whites
on welfare receiving AFDC, food stamps, or other
public assistance dissolved marriages more
frequently than those not receiving welfare. The
same was not found to be true for low-income
blacks. The remarriage rate of divorced females
was three times greater among those not receiving
AFDC than it was among AFDC recipients. This
occurred among both low-income blacks and
whites. The study was designed to find out
whether welfare programs, originally designed to
help needy families, actually dissolved families.

16-3. Berlin, Sharon B., and Linda E. Jones. "Life After
            Welfare: AFDC Termination Among
            Long-Term Recipients." Social Service
            Review 57 (1983): 378-402.

        This article reports on what happens to
white women in smaller cities who become

ineligible for welfare when their youngest child
reaches 18. There is little in the employment
histories of most women in the sample to suggest
they would be able to compete successfully for
jobs that provide them a living wage. The women
reported additional emotional stress as they
juggled payments and skipped medical
appointments since they had no means of paying
for health care. Most women were able to find a
means of livelihood either through work or family
support, social security, or general assistance.
Their incomes were marginal, their health poor,
and their sense of well-being lower than the norm.

16-4.   Bernstein, Blanche. <u>The Politics of Welfare: The
New York City Experience</u>. Cambridge,
MA: Abt Books, 1982.

Bernstein has long been a critic of
legislative and implementation initiatives in
welfare which have led to fraud and the swelling
of welfare rolls and the consequent disincentives
to work and independence. Reviewing public
assistance and related work programs, child
support, and food stamp programs since the
sixties, Bernstein finds that there is a reluctance to
enforce family responsibility and a rejection of the
obligation to work on the part of the welfare
community among many welfare officials, most
black political leaders, the liberal white
community, and the courts. A new agenda is
needed to counteract trends toward family
instability instead of simply continuing to support
female-headed families.

16-5. Cassetty, Judith H., and Ruth McRoy. "Gender, Race, and the Shrinking Welfare Dollar." Public Welfare 41 (Summer 1983): 36-39.

The past decade has witnessed the liberation of women and the rising numbers of women in poverty. Households headed by minority males had seen economic improvement by 1978, as the demand for minority male workers and wage rates increased. Female-headed households did not fare as well in this period. While one out of three households headed by white women remained below the poverty level in both 1965 and 1978, two out of three households headed by minority women were still poor. Educational and employment opportunities improved the pretransfer poverty standing of households headed by minority men by 53 percent; minority women household heads saw a 15 percent improvement.

16-6. Chrissinger, Marlene Sonju. "Factors Affecting Employment of Welfare Mothers." Social Work 25 (1980): 52-56.

The author cites earlier studies that report that while welfare mothers want the same things others do, e.g., a good education and a nice place to live, and that they are equally committed to the work ethic, they lack confidence in their ability to find and keep a job. Welfare mothers who were more frequently employed were better informed about the ratio between earnings and welfare and the real costs of food and health care. It was not clear from the study if mothers limited their employment in order to stay on welfare. Neither education nor employment influenced their labor-market activity. Chrissinger concludes that women will not view work as an alternative to welfare but as a means of achieving a higher standard of living when earnings are combined with other income sources.

16-7. Danziger, Sandra K. "Post-Program Changes in the Lives of AFDC Supported Work Participants: A Qualitative Assessment." Journal of Human Resources 16 (1981): 637-648.

Reporting on a job program for a target AFDC group which was designed to counter the dependency effects of welfare, Danziger says participants had better employment records, steadier jobs with higher wages and fringe benefits as well as increased self-confidence and independence. The program, Supported Work, provided transition from welfare to steady employment for some, transitional opportunity for others, and a positive experience for those who remained on welfare.

16-8. Danziger, Sheldon H., and Kent E. Portney, eds. The Distributional Impacts of Public Policies. New York: St. Martin's, 1988.

These papers discuss the actual benefits and costs of public policies to specific populations. One paper traces the growth of welfare programs under Presidents Nixon and Ford and the cutbacks under Reagan; another reports the peaking of income transfer in the late seventies and the reduction of poverty. Four papers analyze the distributional impacts of proposed changes in child support systems, the impact of cost-of-living adjustments to Social Security benefits, and the distributional impact of taxing unemployment benefits. Another paper describes the effects of transferring income from an absent parent to a child and concludes that this transfer would significantly reduce the poverty of a female-headed family. The remaining chapters discuss tax-related issues.

16-9. Danziger, Sheldon, and others. "Work and Welfare as Determinants of Female Poverty and Household Headship." Quarterly Journal of Economics 97 (1982): 519-534.

Alarm at the growth of female-headed households and the proportion of these households receiving welfare income has raised the question of whether welfare programs encourage families to dissolve by providing benefits primarily to households headed by women. The authors construct a model which allows them to compare the economic benefits available to a woman should she marry or head her own household. Women who choose to be female heads lose income and leisure time. If welfare benefits were reduced, there would be fewer female household heads, but the difference would be relatively small, and there would be a substantial increase in poverty for nonwhites. For nonwhites, the effect of wives working in the market reduces poverty and female headship; for whites, wives working reduces poverty, but increases female headship.

16-10. Danziger, Sheldon H., Irwin Garfinkel, and Robert Haveman. "Poverty, Welfare, and Earnings: A New Approach." Challenge 22 (September/October 1979): 28-34.

Progress in alleviating poverty has been due to extension and increases in public assistance coverage, not to increased wages. Income inequality has remained stable over the last 30 years. If transfer payments were reduced, measured poverty and income inequality would rise substantially. The authors urge the following reforms in public transfer programs: encourage work, encourage demand for low-skilled labor, concentrate additional assistance on female family heads and their children, and simplify administration of welfare programs.

16-11. Day, Phyllis J. "Sex-Role Stereotypes and Public
           Assistance." Social Service Review 53
           (1979): 106-115.

           The continuing hostility of society toward
the poor is explained by beliefs in stereotypical
views about minorities, e.g., deviance from work-
ethic expectations (most recipients are believed to
be able-bodied persons who will not work). This
thinking does not explain the different treatment
of men and women on welfare with regard to
work requirements or the concern for the sexual
morality of women on welfare.

16-12. Dickinson, Nancy S. "Which Welfare Work
           Strategies Work?" Social Work 31
           (1986): 266-272.

           Dickinson asks what welfare work
initiatives will enable recipients to move off
welfare into the labor market and support their
families. The policies of the federal government
indicate an ambivalence towards requiring work
for AFDC mothers. Under Reagan, the Omnibus
Budget Reconciliation Act of 1981 (OBRA)
drastically reduced work incentives. Dickinson
reviews the workfare programs in California and
Utah which are aimed at reducing welfare
dependency and costs by requiring participants to
work off AFDC benefits for no extra pay.
Unfortunately, most people do not participate and
are excused by social workers. Job programs
need to emphasize job development as much as
the employability of participants, and until they
do, workfare programs will have limited success.

16-13. Diehl, Rita, and Beverly Leopold McDonald. "Women and Welfare." Clearinghouse Review 11 (1981): 1036-1041.

The majority of American women are in economic jeopardy throughout their adult lives. As of March 1978, 10.5 million women were living below the poverty level. The structural reasons for this poverty are women's major role in childbearing, childrearing, and homemaking, fluctuating labor-market demands, and discriminatory wage structures. For women who work full time, the wages paid to them gave them a marginal standard of living. Others who move in and out of the labor market because of family responsibilities were dependent on transfer payments and assistance from an outside source not directly related to their labor. The punitive aspects of welfare for the poor mother reflect the values which assign appropriate roles and behavior for women. Without viable alternatives, the present system serves to maintain the economic dependency of most women.

16-14. Ellwood, David T., and Lawrence H. Summers. "Is Welfare Really the Problem?" Public Interest 83 (Spring 1986): 57-78.

The poverty issue has generated dissatisfaction with current policy. The Right finds fault with the poor and the Left with government action or inaction. However, the authors' review of existing policies indicates that although the policies may appear to be haphazard, they do work reasonably well, considering the resources devoted to them. Although current welfare programs do not help people to achieve self-sufficiency, it is unlikely that they have caused the social problems attending poverty. There are few successful programs promoting self-sufficiency among welfare mothers, and society is increasingly unwilling to support welfare dependence even though it encourages mothers to stay home and care for children. Further, social welfare policies cannot be shown to erode the work ethic on black male youth, as they are not eligible for most of the programs. The authors conclude that "government policies cannot be blamed for a great deal of the problems of the disadvantaged."

16-15. Ellwood David T., and Mary-Jo Bane. "The Impact of AFDC On Family Structure and Living Arrangements." Research in Labor Economics 7 (1985): 137-207.

Much blame is cast upon the welfare system, particularly the Aid to Families with Dependent Children (AFDC) program, as the cause of increased rates of the numbers of female-headed households with children. This blame continues despite the lack of empirical evidence. The authors find that divorce and separation rates for poor women are strongly related to welfare benefit levels. The rates are higher for mothers with children than for married women without children. However, there is no strong link between welfare and births of children to unmarried women. Welfare does influence behavior, particularly the living arrangements of young single mothers who often establish their own homes with welfare housing allowances.

16-16. Farnell, James E., and Elaine Pitzalis. "How Welfare Recipients Find Jobs: A Case Study in New Jersey." Monthly Labor Review 101 (February 1978): 43-45.

The Welfare Board of Monmouth County, New Jersey, found that their welfare recipients, for the most part, used private contacts to secure jobs. Job search characteristics differ by age, sex, and race. Men and older workers used more job search methods than women and younger workers. The largest proportion of recipients found employment in the health and clerical fields. Blacks were more likely to be in health and nonprivate cleaning jobs while only whites obtained professional and technical positions. Full-time employment for women was related to the age of their children; all the men were in full-time jobs.

16-17. Froland, Charles, and Joseph Bell. "Policy Experimentation: Framing the Welfare Debate." Social Service Review 53 (1979): 441-451.

Pointing the way for political debate, the authors review investigations on the incentive effects of a guaranteed annual income in relation to work experiences and family situations of low-income individuals and families. Research will have the greatest impact if framed in terms of political realities. The current welfare debate is based on conflicting values, and this situation is likely to continue.

16-18. Garfinkel, Irwin, ed. Income-Tested Transfer Programs: The Case For and Against. New York: Academic Press, 1982.

Collected here are the papers from a 1979 conference sponsored by the Ford Foundation's Institute for Research on Poverty and the Social Security Administration. The writers question whether income-tested transfer programs stigmatize recipients, creating sharp distinctions between beneficiaries and nonbeneficiaries. These papers challenge the sixties assumption that income-tested programs were superior to non-income-tested programs and suggest reforms which would reduce the role of income testing in the tax-transfer system. The conference concludes that income-testing programs are more likely than non-income-testing programs to stigmatize the poor, but it is not clear whether income testing weakens social cohesion, harms the economic well-being of the poor, or is inefficient in terms of the work output of the poor.

16-19. Goodban, Nancy. "The Psychological Impact of Being on Welfare." Social Service Review 59 (1985): 403-422.

A sampling of black single mothers on AFDC indicated that they were on welfare for temporary, uncontrollable reasons. They experienced extreme psychological and economic hardship and felt trapped, guilty, ashamed, and stigmatized by a society that devalues the poor.

16-20. Gordon, Linda. "What Does Welfare Regulate?" Social Research 55 (Winter 1988): 609-630; also discussion, 631-647.

In their four books since 1971, Frances Fox Piven and Richard A. Cloward have defined the way that radicals think about welfare policy and the welfare-rights movement. They see welfare policy, as it has developed, as a tool of maintaining the social order and the economic system which exploits labor. Gordon offers a gender analysis of these issues and finds that entitlement programs go to men and welfare programs support women. The welfare-rights movement can best be seen as a women's movement and as a feminist movement.

16-21. Hasenfeld, Yeheskel. "Citizens' Encounters with Welfare State Bureaucracies." Social Service Review 59 (1985): 622-635.

Acknowledging that the evolution of citizenship recognizes the social right to an acceptable level of economic welfare according to prevailing norms, state bureaucracies are empowered and funded to respond to citizens' social rights claims. Hasenfeld explains the bureaucratic encounters based on power-dependence; the more resources the client can martial in her encounter with bureaucrats, the more successful will be the results. People who have no resources and are dependent on AFDC are less successful in their encounters than those who depend on Social Security.

16-22. Hoffman, Saul D., and Greg J. Duncan. "A Comparison of Choice-Based Multinomial and Nested Logic-Models: The Family-Structure and Welfare Use Decisions of Divorced or Separated Women." Journal of Human Resources 23 (1988): 550-562.

The researchers were interested in how the receipt of welfare payments influences women's decisions to remarry. In the years following the dissolutions of marriage, while AFDC recipients (both white and black) valued their benefits, receiving benefits did not seem to influence their decision to remarry. Women seem to choose to remain single with or without welfare benefits.

16-23. Kosterlitz, Julie. "Reexamining Welfare: The
President Has Reignited the Welfare
Reform Debate." National Journal 18
(December 6, 1986): 2926-2931.

There is a surprising consensus among
ideological opposites that the minority of
recipients who stay on welfare for long periods of
time should be targeted for greater work
requirements and for the enforcement of support
awards from absentee fathers. Despite almost 20
years of programming for the poor, the number of
poor has remained level. However, the
demographics have changed; there are more
women and children in poverty now than
previously. The numbers of working poor have
increased due to the recession, static minimum
wage and the growth of lower-paying service jobs.
The gap between the rich and poor has grown.
Questioning whether there are enough jobs,
Kosterlitz concludes that work programs alone
cannot solve the problems of the poor.

16-24. Levy, Frank. "The Labor Supply of Female
Household Heads, or AFDC Work
Incentives Don't Work Too Well."
Journal of Human Resources 14 (1979):
76-97.

The findings are ambiguous about
whether work incentives promote the work effort
of AFDC-recipient women who are heads of
households. Levy finds that not only will raising
the basic level of payments lower a woman's
expected work effort but also that greater work
incentives, including lower tax rates, and a more
liberal deductions policy, will lower expected work
hours. "While these incentives may encourage
increased work among women who previously
worked very little the increase will be more than
offset by other women who are induced to cut
back on work."

16-25. Masters, Stanley H. "The Effects of Supported Work on the Earnings and Transfer Payments of its AFDC Target Group." Journal of Human Resources 16 (1981): 600-636.

Masters reviews a work experience program originally developed for ex-addicts and its use with AFDC recipients who had little training and wanted to work. The paper discusses the increased earnings of the participants and its positive, long-lasting effect on earnings of the AFDC participants after the program.

16-26. Murray, Charles. Losing Ground: American Social Policy, 1950-1980. New York: Basic, 1984.

Murray argues that the government made a strategic error in its social policy by "making it profitable for the poor to behave in the short term in ways that were destructive in the long term." He traces the revolution in social spending from the 1950's through 1980 and discusses causes for the growing numbers of poor despite increased federal expenditures: increased unemployment among working-aged males, and increasing numbers of female-headed families--not just as a proportion of families in poverty, but also in absolute numbers. Murray proposes that all legislation and court decisions that treat people differently based on race be repealed, and that a voucher system for education be established. He also calls for the total elimination of the federal welfare and income-support structure for working-aged people which lead to "great disruption in expectations and accustomed goals."

16-27. Murray, Charles, and Deborah Laren. "According
to Age: Longitudinal Profiles of AFDC
Recipients and the Poor by Age Group."
American Enterprise Institute for Public
Policy Research and Marquette
University Institute for Family Studies.
1986. (ERIC microfiche ED280908)

This report, sponsored by the American
Enterprise Institute for the Working Seminar on
the Family and American Welfare Policy, was
aided by a life-span study begun in 1968. It builds
on Greg Duncan's work "Years of Poverty, Years
of Plenty" (Ann Arbor, Institute for Social
Research) in which poverty is found to be a
temporary condition, and welfare recipiency a
temporary response. Murray compares his own
rise from a poverty-stricken graduate student with
a family to support to the families described by
Duncan, and says it is hard to stay in poverty if
one completes high school, stays with a job, and
avoids having babies.

16-28. Nichols, Abigail C. "Why Welfare Mothers Work:
Implications for Employment and
Training Services." Social Service Review
53 (1979): 378-391.

Although Congress has made it clear that
it wants low-income single mothers to work rather
than to rely solely on public welfare, it wants their
working to be voluntary. Studying working and
nonworking AFDC mothers in a California
community, this study reports how the allocation
of social services can increase employment,
support for education, training, and career
orientation, and strengthen the self-support ethic.
High enough wages will lure most single mothers
into the work force. This study did not show
greater child-care problems among nonworking
compared with working mothers.

16-29. O'Neill, June. "Transfers and Poverty: Cause
and/or Effect?" CATO Journal 6
(Spring/Summer 1986): 55-83.

The public is concerned about the
resurgence of high levels of poverty and the
growth of the public transfer sector of the
economy. Is there a relationship? O'Neill
believes that economic growth and the business
cycle are major determinants of the change in
poverty. The growth of welfare, e.g., Aid to
families with Dependent Children, is due to the
increase of female-headed families. O'Neill
concludes that welfare alleviates poverty in the
short term, but in the long term it fosters
dependency and impedes the upward mobility of
families.

16-30. Pearldaughter, Andia M., and Vivian Schneider.
"Women and Welfare." Golden Gate
University Law Review 3 (1980): 1043-
1046.

Women are second-class economic
citizens whether they choose to work in the home
or in the marketplace. Homemakers, although
legally entitled to support and maintenance from
spouses, are unable to enforce this right. They
are disproportionately represented among welfare
recipients; welfare offers them no escape from
poverty. Until sexism, the root cause of much of
this country's poverty, is attacked, welfare rolls
will continue to swell. The welfare system with its
workfare provisions maintains a continuing supply
of low-wage workers who are primarily women.
A vicious cycle is therefore created whereby
women, because of their marginal labor-force
position and unequal position in marriage, are
much more likely than men to enter the welfare
system from which they are fed back into the
secondary economy.

16-31. Sanger, Mary Bryna. "Generating Employment for
        AFDC Mothers." Social Service Review
        58 (1984): 28-48.

Though the policy of the Reagan
Administration is to move people off of welfare
and into work, various employment programs have
been disappointing, and it remains difficult for
AFDC mothers to make the transition. Sanger
reviews a new program, grant diversion, which
seeks to create jobs for welfare mothers and to
provide incentives to both employers and
employees.

16-32. Schram, Sanford F., and others. "Child Poverty
        and Welfare Benefits: A Reassessment
        with State Data of the Claim that
        American Welfare Breeds Dependence."
        American Journal of Economics and
        Society 47 (1988): 409-422.

Statistical data does not support those
critics of the American welfare system who claim
that welfare exacerbates poverty by making living
on welfare preferable to overcoming poverty, and
that high welfare benefits attract families onto
welfare and increase the number of children living
in poverty. There is little evidence that individuals
choose poverty and thereby condemn their
children to poverty. Rather, explanations for
poverty are related to general economic factors.

16-33. Spakes, Patricia. "Mandatory Work Registration for
        Welfare Parents: A Family Impact
        Analysis." Journal of Marriage and the
        Family 44 (1982): 685-700.

Interested in the contradictory nature of
the literature on American family policies, Spakes
investigates the mandatory work registration
requirement and its impact on AFDC families in

Wisconsin. She finds that the requirement often has negative consequences for the families, who reported additional stress when having to look for work, lowered self-esteem when unable to obtain employment, increased family tension arising from inadequate child care and supervision of older children, and disappointment at the lack of training. Those who were already looking for a job or who had found employment reported positively on the mandatory registration requirement.

16-34. Spivey, W. Allen. "Problems and Paradoxes in Economic and Social Policies of Modern Welfare States." Annals of the American Academy of Political and Social Science 479 (1985): 14-30.

Reviewing modern European welfare polices as well as those of Japan, the United States, and Canada, Spivey finds that the sixties saw expansion and commitment whereas the seventies brought constriction as a result of rising inflation, unemployment, the OPEC oil crisis, and increased government deficits. Under Reagan and Thatcher, the limits of the welfare state have been explored as austere social welfare budgets were adopted here and throughout Western Europe. Although the author sees economic recovery for most of these nations, the aging of their populations and relatively high unemployment rates coupled with low real economic growth rates will continue to exact pressures on social welfare programs.

16-35. Treas, Judith. "Trickle Down or Transfers?
Postwar Determinants of Family Income
Inequality." American Sociological
Review 48 (1983): 546-559.

Work and welfare are the two widely
recognized approaches to bettering the lot of low-
income Americans. Welfare or government
assistance programs favor public income transfers
to the poor; work emphasizes the creation of
more jobs, thus encouraging a trickle-down effect.
Preferring to cut both taxes and social welfare
programs, the Reagan Administration has stressed
the distributional benefits of the trickle-down
effect.   However, families headed by women do
not benefit from the trickle-down approach.
Public transfer programs have been more effective
for reducing inequality, especially for family types
at great risk to poverty, e.g., female-headed
families.

16-36. U.S. Senate. Committee on Finance. Data and
Materials Related to Welfare Programs
for Families with Children. 100th
Congress, 2nd Session. Washington, DC:
Government Printing Office, 1987.
(Y 4.F 49:S.prt. 100-101)

For each welfare program (Aid to
Families with Dependent Children, child support
and establishment of paternity, employment and
training for AFDC recipients, health programs,
and federal tax policies), the report includes a
brief description of major provisions and then
many tables of statistics. Data include such
information as maximum AFDC benefits by family
size; and average income tax liability and tax rate
in 1988 under prior Law and under the 1986 Act.
Many tables are designed to show the effects of
the Reagan budget and tax policies. Part VIII,
Selected Income, Wage and Population Data,

includes statistics and such topics as persons and families below the poverty level.

16-37. U.S. Senate. Committee on Labor and Human Resources. Work and Welfare. 99th Congress, 2nd Session. Washington, DC: Government Printing Office, 1986. (Y 4. L 11/4: S. prt. 99-177)

This report traces the history of employment and training programs for welfare recipients, beginning with the New Deal, through the War on Poverty, and the Nixon and Carter welfare reform proposals. Chapters cover major issues in work and welfare policy, such as: "Should AFDC recipients be treated as employable?", "How should employment and training programs be administered", "What should be the nature of an employment and training program: job search, workfare, classroom training?", and "What about child care?" The bulk of the report details (with numerous footnotes) the history of AFDC legislation through 1985.

16-38. Weidman, John C., Richard N. White., and B. Katherine Swartz. "Training Women on Welfare for 'High-Tech' Jobs: Results from a Demonstration Program." Evaluation and Program Planning 11 (1988): 105-114.

Welfare mothers participating in the Work Incentive Program (WIN), which seeks to move them off welfare into self-sustaining jobs, were trained to be electronic technicians and enjoyed support services, which included child care, transportation, counseling, medical care, on-the-job training, and job placement. Nonetheless, only 29 percent of the WIN-sponsored women completed the training, and only 64 percent of these graduates found jobs. The savings to

taxpayers of those who became independent of
WIN and welfare were considered to justify the
initial high cost of training and to caution state
governments not to emphasize job placement over
job training, even though the 1981 Omnibus
Budget Reconciliation Act requires some sort of
work as a condition of receiving welfare benefits.

16-39. "Welfare and Poverty Among Children."
Congressional Research Service Review 8
(1987): 1-23.

Prepared by the research branch of the
Library of Congress, this publication is intended
to present selected research and analysis to
members of Congress. It includes brief articles on
topics such as welfare reform, Medicaid, child-
support enforcement, housing, work incentives and
disincentives, welfare and family structure,
workfare, and teen parenting. The articles include
information such as statistics, research results,
past policy, and policy options.

17 Welfare Reform and Workfare

After nearly two decades of debate on welfare reform, Congress passed the Family Support Act (Public Law 100-485) in 1988. Senator Daniel P. Moynihan (D-NY), chief sponsor of the legislation, was an advisor to President Richard Nixon in 1969 when the administration proposed a Family Assistance Plan (FAP) that would have set a nationwide minimum benefit for AFDC (Aid to Families with Dependent Children) recipients. FAP never got through Congress. President Jimmy Carter also tried to reform the welfare system. He proposed a Program for Better Jobs and Income, which was also defeated in Congress.

By the mid-eighties consensus had developed that welfare reform was necessary and that the system should emphasize training and employment rather than income maintenance. As finally passed, the law represented a compromise between conservatives, who got the workfare provisions they wanted, and liberals, who managed to gain benefits for two-parent families, money for state education and training programs, and child-care and medical benefits for welfare recipients who find jobs.

The provisions of the act reflect conservative beliefs in work for welfare and in fathers having the obligation to pay child support. The Act established the Family Support Program (FSP) which replaced Aid to Families with Dependent Children (AFDC). FSP requires nonexempt recipients to enroll in a work, education or training program, and to work their way off welfare. Its target group is female heads of households, and it has been designed to prevent welfare dependency and to foster employment. The welfare-to-work provision is the heart of the new law and is to be put in place by the states by October 1, 1990. It includes child support and Medicaid assistance while the family makes the transition from welfare to work. The legislation provides money to carry out the program for the first five years. FSP requires employers automatically to deduct child-support payments from the paycheck of the absent parent, and it requires all states to extend welfare benefits to families in which both parents are unemployed.

Specific provisions of the legislation include:

--Single parents on welfare with children over three have to participate in a new Job Opportunities and Basic Skills (JOBS) program offering education, training, and work activities.

--One adult in each two-parent welfare household will have to participate in a job search. If the parent doesn't find work, she or he will be required to work 16 hours a week in a state-organized job. A young parent could work instead toward a high school diploma.

--States will have to concentrate available resources on the toughest cases: young parents without a high school education, long-term recipients, and families with older children who are expected to lose eligibility.

--JOBS participants will receive transportation and child-care help, and parents working their way off welfare will qualify for a year of transitional child-care and Medicaid benefits. States could charge for the transitional services on a sliding scale.

--The federal government will require, for the first time, that all states pay cash benefits to two-parent welfare families.

--States will have to step up child-support collections from noncustodial parents, including automatic wage withholding for court-awarded support payments. States will get federal money to set up a computerized tracking and monitoring system for child-support enforcement.

The welfare revolution expected under FSP will unfold gradually at best since only half of those on welfare can feasibly be required to take part in a work program because of legitimate reasons such as illness, children at home under the age of three, and aging or handicapped dependents. For states with similar welfare-to-work programs in place, the FSP funding will mean an increase in funding for education and training programs, medical insurance, and child-care expenses. Senator Moynihan commented that we are removing the stigma from people on welfare, no longer treating them as "undeserving leeches ... we are finally defining these people as unemployed, and that's a breakthrough." (William K. Stevens, "Welfare Bill: Historic Scope But a Gradual Impact," New York Times, 2 October 1988, p. 20, col. 1.)

17-1. "After Years of Debate, Welfare Reform Clears."
      <u>Congressional Quarterly Almanac 1988</u>.
      Washington, DC: Congressional
      Quarterly, 1989, pp. 349-364.

    This article outlines provisions of the
1988 welfare reform law and gives a brief history
of 1969 and 1977 attempts at reform. It describes
the legislative history of the act and analyzes
public and Congressional support, both liberal and
conservative.

17-2. Brockway, George P. "Reality and Welfare
      Reform." <u>New Leader</u> 71 (November 28,
      1988): 14-16.

    The low cost of Senator Moynihan's (D-
NY) new Family Security Act indicates its modest
ambitions: $3.34 billion over five years, $668
million a year, $20.62 for every person living in
poverty in the U.S.--about one-third of the
projected cost of the next space shuttle. Congress
clearly has no intention of doing anything about
poverty, the working poor, the homeless, the
hungry, and those in need of health care. The
solution is not workfare but jobs.

17-3. Butler, Stuart, and Anna Kondratas. <u>Out of the
      Poverty Trap: A Conservative Strategy for
      Welfare Reform</u>. New York: Free Press,
      1987.

    Butler and Kondratas analyze what they
see as the inherent flaws in the Great Society
programs. In the chapter on welfare and the
family they argue that long-term welfare reform
has to focus on strengthening the two-parent
family. Their proposals include tax reform (the
earned income credit, for example), elimination of
regulations on homework and child-care facilities,
forcing grandparents to support minor children's

offspring, workfare programs, and an explicit limit on the length of AFDC eligibility.

17-4. Caputo, Richard K. "Limits of Welfare Reform." Social Casework 70 (1989): 85-95.

The structural shifts in the economy-- from urban areas as centers of producing goods to centers of information processing--have been accompanied by changes in the size and composition of the urban employment base, causing a mismatch in high-wage employment for many inner-city residents. The link between work strategies and welfare policy requires the federal government to raise the minimum wage, improve tax policies, remove employment obstacles, find and create jobs, and to link welfare reform with strategies for finding jobs.

17-5. Cottingham,˙Phoebe H., and David T. Ellwood, eds. Welfare Policy for the 1990s. Cambridge, MA: Harvard University Press, 1989.

Essays discussing the circumstances that led to the passage of the welfare reform bill in 1988. The authors consider public policy questions such as whether economic independence is a realistic objective for significant numbers of those currently receiving welfare, how to reduce poverty among young unmarried mothers and their children, the persistent poverty of the inner city, the efficacy of workfare programs, and changes in the child-support system.

17-6. Coughlin, Richard M. <u>Reforming Welfare:</u>
<u>Lessons, Limits, and Choices.</u>
Albuquerque, NM: University of New
Mexico Press, 1989.

A collection of essays on various aspects
of welfare reform, including ideology and welfare
reform, the efficacy of workfare programs, a
reform proposal from the National Coalition on
Women, Work and Welfare Reform, and a
chapter describing welfare myths and stereotypes
and their impact on welfare reform.

17-7. Ellwood, David T. <u>Divide and Conquer:</u>
<u>Responsible Security for America's Poor.</u>
Occasional Paper No. 1, Ford Foundation
Project on Social Welfare and the
American Future. New York: Ford
Foundation, 1987.

Ellwood demonstrates that long-term
poverty is intimately related to family structure,
though other problems such as unemployment
cannot be overlooked. He offers suggestions to
help the working poor, such as increased medical
insurance, an increase in the minimum wage, an
earned income tax credit, and transitional support
for the unemployed. Ellwood includes a chapter
on families headed by women in which he
discusses why single mothers are poor, whether
they should be required to work or be allowed to
stay home with young children, and describes the
child-support assurance plan being tried in
Wisconsin.

17-8. Handler, Joel F. "Consensus on Redirection - Which Direction?" Focus 11 (1988): 29-34.

Handler describes the new consensus on changes to AFDC and notes the emphasis on responsibility, education, and training. He traces the history of AFDC and says that there has always been hostility to female-headed families in poverty and that new proposals show the reemergence of that hostility.

17-9. Hylton, Richard D. "The New Welfare Bill: When More Isn't Enough." Black Enterprise 19 (January 1989): 1.

Congressional compromise has produced a half-hearted attempt at welfare reform. The new bill requires single parents on welfare with children older than three to participate in job and basic skills training. In a two-parent family on welfare, at least one adult would have to participate in a job search. Critics claim that workfare punishes people on welfare and does not lead to full-time jobs. Since the states have enormous leeway in providing education and training, the new bill will likely increase the unequal way poor people are treated.

17-10. Karger, Howard Jacob, and David Stoesz. "Welfare Reform: Maximum Feasible Exaggeration." Tikkun 4 (March/April 1989): 23-25, 118-122.

The authors claim that "the Family Support Act of 1988 is at best a feeble attempt at welfare reform, and at worst harsh and punitive". The so-called reform measure is harsh and punitive in its requirement that at least one family member spend at least 16 hours per week in an unpaid job in return for benefits, in its measures

to establish paternity, and in the requirement that
child-support payments be automatically deducted
from paychecks. It is feeble in that "44 percent of
the new jobs created under Reagan were part-
time service-sector jobs that paid less than $7,400
per year" and which relegated jobholders to the
ranks of the working poor. Karger and Stoesz
attribute the pressure for welfare reform to the
challenge of the federal government's role in
social welfare by both conservative and liberal
intellectuals, to the rise of the traditionalist
movement, and to the deficit-driven federal
budget.

17-11. Kirk, David L. "The California Work/Welfare
        Scheme." Public Interest 83 (Spring
        1986): 34-48.

        In 1985, California passed the Greater
Avenues to Independence (GAIN) program
designed to provide welfare recipients with a
reasonable level of benefits and maintain
incentives to work without spending at politically
unacceptable levels. California became convinced
that although training is costly, moving people off
welfare for longer periods made economic sense.
GAIN provides high levels of support with
sanctions against those who break the rules.
Training, counseling, commutation fares, and
after-school child care are provided. Kirk is
enthusiastic about the value of the struggle for
independence and a paying job in breaking the
cycle of dependency and despondency
characteristic of long-term welfare recipients.

17-12. Lerman, Robert I. "Nonwelfare Approaches to Helping the Poor." Focus 11 (1988): 24-28.

Recent proposals for restructuring the welfare system "place too much faith in the ability of welfare reforms to make welfare recipients into high-earning workers." Lerman proposes a bridge program that would help low-income families live decently outside the welfare system; it would include a child-support assurance program, a refundable child tax credit, a wage rate subsidy for family heads, state health insurance programs to replace and supplement Medicaid, and enhanced training for those remaining on welfare. Such a system would appeal to taxpayers because it would help reduce poverty without expanding welfare programs associated with dependency and the nondeserving poor.

17-13. Mead, Lawrence M. "The Logic of Workfare: The Underclass and Work Policy." Annals of the American Academy of Political and Social Science 501: 156-169.

Mead argues that workfare is seen as a solution today because the prevailing view is that traditional barriers to opportunity, e.g., lack of jobs and discrimination are no longer as formidable. The new job of public policy is not to remove barriers but to overcome the culture of poverty. Mead believes that workfare programs should set high minimum participation rates and should be directed at men as well as women. Workfare programs embody the culture's belief that "both education and work are public activities to be expected of all competent citizens, for their own good and society's" (p. 160).

17-14. Miller, Dorothy C. "AFDC: Mapping a Strategy
for Tomorrow." Social Service Review 57
(1983): 599-613.

Aid to Families with Dependent Children,
created in 1935, has had so many problems that
the tendency is to try and work with pieces of the
program rather than look at the whole. Under
Reagan, the Omnibus Budget Reconciliation Act
(OBRA) of 1981 made some detrimental changes
in AFDC. One of the most devastating was a
reversal of the work incentive provisions. This
legislation reflects the antiwelfare bias of the
Reagan Administration against women and
children who are no longer considered the worthy
poor. It is imbued with sexism and reflects the
"misogynist backlash to the women's movement"
and racism, as taxpayers perceive large numbers
of minority women receiving assistance. Future
strategies should protect AFDC and related
programs, improve AFDC, create ways for
families to leave the program, and prevent the
conditions that force families to go on welfare.

17-15. The New Consensus on Family and Welfare.
Report of the Working Seminar on
Family and American Welfare Policy.
Washington, DC: American Enterprise
Institute, 1987.

Prepared by experts from various
backgrounds and viewpoints, this report describes
the poor in terms of race, age, and family
composition. The report's focus is on behavioral
dependency and on the family as the primary
place to teach children to become productive
citizens. It recommends workfare, a time limit on
eligibility for AFDC, tax changes to benefit the
working poor, and flexibility in state and local
implementation of welfare policies.

17-16. Pope, Jacqueline. "Women and Welfare Reform."
Black Scholar 19 (May/June 1988): 22-30.

Poverty management continues to be the
goal of welfare policy. In a nation that professes
to care about children and families, public
assistance appears to impoverish children, punish
heads of families, and embody bias against the
poor. As more and more families fall below the
poverty line, they are not entitled to benefits and
the secure family life that is ensured to the middle
class through public policy. Pope recommends an
Economic Security Plan that encompasses a
minimum standard of living, employment, a social
salary for parenting, universal child and medical
care, a housing tax reform, child support, an
improved minimum wage, and the elimination of
racism, sexism, and ageism.

17-17. Riemer, David Raphael. The Prisoners of Welfare:
Liberating America's Poor from
Unemployment and Low Wages. New
York: Praeger, 1988.

Riemer treats all poor as a single group
and does not discuss women in poverty
specifically. He proposes to eliminate the current
welfare system entirely, since "it does not cause
poverty, but by its design it fails to eliminate
poverty". (p. 8) He would instead provide cash
payments to those who cannot work in order to
put them above the poverty line, offer community
service jobs to those who can work, and provide
the working poor with sufficient supplements to
boost them above the poverty line. In addition to
his policy proposals, Riemer includes chapters on
the definition of the poor, the job shortage, low-
wage jobs, AFDC, and the right not to be poor.

17-18. Rover, Julie. "Welfare Reform: The Next
Domestic Priority?" Congressional
Quarterly Weekly Report 44 (September
27, 1986): 2281-2288.

In 1986, Democrats in the House of
Representatives issued a report, "The Road to
Independence: Strengthening America's families in
need," which recommended greater emphasis on
helping the working poor and educating and
training those on welfare to enter the work force.
The article summarizes the history of Aid to
Families with Dependent Children (AFDC) and
highlights its illogic, i.e., rewarding absent fathers
by supporting their children and penalizing AFDC
mothers who go to work by reducing their public
assistance and eliminating their free access to
health care provided by Medicaid.

17-19. Salaman, Lester M., ed. Welfare, the Elusive
Consensus. New York: Praeger, 1978.

The consensus on the need for welfare
reform does not translate into action because of
the complexity of the system, fear of less generous
programs, the suspected impact on the work ethic,
and political opposition. The authors of the
essays included in this book discuss the grand
design of public assistance, the dynamics of
welfare dependency, welfare program
administration, and welfare and American values.

17-20. U.S. Congress. House. Committee on Ways and
Means. Family Welfare Reform Act.
100th Congress, 1st Session. Washington,
DC: Government Printing Office, 1988.
(Y 4.W 36:100-38)

This hearing was held to consider a
proposal to replace the AFDC system with a new
family support program (FSP). Witnesses discuss

the need for reform and address specific
components of the proposed legislation, including
a national education, training and work
(NETWORK) program, reimbursement of child-
care expenses, work incentives, and child-support
enforcement and paternity determination
procedures.

17-21. U.S. Congress. House. Committee on Ways and
          Means. General Explanation of the
          Family Support Act of 1988. 101st
          Congress, 1st Session. Washington, DC:
          Government Printing Office, 1989.
          (Y 4.W 36:WMCP 101-3)

          This is a general overview of the Family
Support Act of 1988 (Public Law 100-485),
describing its requirements, then explaining some
of the provisions of the law, such as establishment
of paternity, more fully. It includes effective dates
for provisions of the law and concludes with a
summary of the estimated cost to the federal
government for FY 1989-FY 1993 and estimates
for numbers of families affected when provisions
are fully effective.

17-22. U.S. Congress. House. Committee on Ways and
          Means. How to Help the Working Poor;
          and Problems of the Working Poor.
          101st Congress, 1st Session. Washington,
          DC: Government Printing Office, 1989.
          (Y 4.W 36:101-5)

          In 1987, more than half of America's
poor lived in a households in which at least one
member of that household worked. This hearing
explores the remedies which would eliminate the
phrase "working poor". Possible remedies include
expansion of the earned income tax credit (EITC),
which since it is available only to working parents
who live with and support their children, is viewed

as both pro-work and pro-family. Other remedies include changes in the dependent care tax credit and an increase in the minimum wage.

17-23. U.S. Congress. House. Committee on Ways and Means. Welfare Reform. 100th Congress, 1st Session. Washington, DC: Government Printing Office, 1987. (Y 4.W 36:100-14)

The committee held hearings to examine various proposals for reforming the federal welfare system. Witnesses testified on such issues as child support, job training, workfare programs in several states, and the problem of behavioral dependency.

17-24. U.S. Congress. House. Committee on Ways and Means. Work, Education and Training Opportunities for Welfare Recipients. 99th Congress, 2nd Session. Washington, DC: Government Printing Office, 1986. (Y 4.W 36:99-91)

Includes testimony on the National Governors' Association's policy position that in order to ensure equity, a comprehensive national income security program is needed, fully funded by the national government, and providing equitable treatment across state lines. The governors also believe that most welfare recipients can and want to work. Another portion of the hearing describes state legislative initiatives that address the issues of teenage pregnancy and parenting. The Child Welfare League of America submitted information on possible reform measures, stressing the importance of a voluntary workfare program and the need for adequate child care for those mothers who choose to participate. Also includes submission from Isabel Sawhill, "Does Welfare Undermine the Family?," in which she describes welfare as a minor factor in the growth of female-headed families and advocates programs that would promote the stability of the family.

17-25. U.S. Congress. Senate. Committee on Finance. Welfare: Reform or Replacement? (Child Support Enforcement). Parts I and II. 100th Congress, 1st Session. Washington, DC: Government Printing Office, 1987. (Y 4.F 49:S.hrg. 100-335, S.hrg. 100-395)

This hearing was held to consider changes in the welfare program. Witnesses from federal, state, and local governments and organizations such as the National Urban League and the Children's Defense Fund discuss various strategies for welfare reform, concentrating on the need for stricter child-support enforcement.

17-26. U.S. Congress. Senate. Committee on Finance. Welfare: Reform or Replacement? (Short-Term v. Long-Term Dependency). 100th Congress, 1st Session. Washington, DC: Government Printing Office, 1988. (Y 4.F 49:S.hrg. 100-484)

Another in a series of hearings held to examine proposed changes in the federal welfare system. Witnesses describe the problems with the current system and review studies that examine the problem of behavioral dependency among welfare recipients.

17-27. U.S. Congress. Senate. Committee on Finance.
<u>Welfare: Reform or Replacement?</u> (Work
and Welfare). 100th Congress, 1st
Session. Washington, DC: Government
Printing Office, 1988. (Y 4.F 49:S.hrg.
100-320)

This hearing focuses on proposed changes
in federal work requirements for welfare
recipients. The committee members heard
testimony on workfare programs in several states,
as well as discussion on whether or not such
programs should be mandatory for AFDC
recipients.

17-28. U.S. Congressional Budget Office. <u>Work-Related</u>
<u>Programs for Welfare Recipients</u>.
Washington, DC: Congressional Budget
Office, 1987. (Y 10.2:W 89/2)

When Aid to Families with Dependent
Children (AFDC) was created in 1935, it was
intended to assist fatherless families so that
mothers could stay home and devote their time to
childrearing. Now, however, policymakers want to
reduce welfare dependency by helping AFDC
mothers become self-sufficient through paid
employment. The Congressional Budget Office
studied options for work-related programs,
examining factors such as the changing role of
women in America and the costs of such
programs. It assessed previous federal programs
and several state programs and found that such
programs have "repeatedly been shown to be
effective in increasing the average earnings of
economically disadvantaged female participants"
(p. 43). The report concludes with a discussion of
issues for Congress to consider: eligibility
requirements, target participation levels,
performance standards, priorities among
recipients, and levels of federal funding.

17-29. U.S. Domestic Policy Council. Low Income
        Opportunity Working Group. <u>Up From
        Dependency: A New National Public
        Assistance Strategy</u>. Washington, DC:
        Government Printing Office, 1987. (PrEx
        15.2:D 44).

       In his 1986 State of the Union address,
President Reagan charged the White House
Domestic Policy Council to prepare "an evaluation
of programs and a strategy for immediate action
to meet the financial, educational, social, and
safety concerns of poor families. I am talking
about real and lasting emancipation, because the
success of welfare should be judged by how many
of its recipients become independent of welfare."
The working group interviewed scholars, federal
workers, welfare recipients, ex-recipients, and
welfare workers. This volume presents the
group's recommendations which, in general, rely
on community- and state-based projects. The
report also includes brief chapters on poverty and
welfare programs and the potential for reform,
topics which are discussed in more detail in
supplemental volumes (see #17-30).

17-30. U.S. Interagency Low Income Opportunity
        Advisory Board. <u>Up From Dependency:
        A New National Public Assistance
        Strategy</u>. Supplements 1-4. Washington,
        DC: Government Printing Office, 1987.
        (PrEx 15.2:D 44/supps.)

       Supplements to the report (see #17-29).
Supplement 1, Volume 1 contains an overview of
the current public assistance system. Volumes 2
and 3 of Supplement 1 contain descriptions of 59
major low-income assistance programs.
Supplement 2 ("Experiments in Reform") was
never distributed to depository libraries.
Supplement 3, reflecting the Reagan
Administration's faith in self-help programs,

contains descriptions of 385 programs that feature
active involvement of members of the low income
population. Supplement 4 provides a overview of
research on welfare and poverty.

17-31. Walsh, Joan. "Fighting Poverty After Reagan."
Nation 248 (March 13, 1989): 336-39.

For anyone concerned with poverty in the
United States, the best thing to be said about the
Reagan era is that it is over. Conservatives,
fueled by David Stockman's budget figures and
Charles Murray's Losing Ground, set back
antipoverty forces. Today, these groups are
smarter, are targeting the problems that affect
poor children, and are tightening priorities:
increases in the minimum wage, expansion of
government health insurance, a more generous
earned income tax credit, and other help for low-
income workers.

17-32. "Welfare Reform: Pro and Con." Congressional
Digest 67 (February 1988): 33-64.

This issue, devoted to the pros and cons
of welfare reform, focuses on one program, Aid to
Families With Dependent Children (AFDC). In
1987, the House of Representatives passed the
Family Welfare Reform Act which would have
replaced AFDC with a family support program,
offering workfare and a safety net. Rep. Thomas
J. Downey (D-NY) argues in favor of passage,
saying that the act targets the use of public money
for long-term welfare dependents and provides
transitional services and reduces the barriers for
people who want to work. Rep. Bill Frenzel (R-
MN) asserts that this is another Democratic Party
attempt to put someone's hands in someone else's
pocket, and it will expand the welfare rolls and be
too costly.

17-33. Wiseman, Michael. "How Workfare Really
Works." Public Interest 89 (Fall 1987):
36-47.

Wiseman declares workfare a new kind of
welfare fraud. He finds that current AFDC
operations do a good job of providing income
support to families who meet the eligibility
requirements. He knows of no successful large-
scale workfare program including the often-touted
California Community Work Experience Program.
It has to be understood that workfare will not
make welfare go away because the scope of
workfare programs is too narrow. The long-term
reduction of welfare dependency requires child-
suppport enforcement, tax credits, improved
public education, and health care.

17-34. Wright, Daniel. "Workfare: A Fine Idea in Need
of Work." Fortune, October 24, 1988,
213+.

Congress must pay attention to the
lessons of past welfare reforms by setting up a
program that will not be subverted by government
bureaucracies. Strict principles of accountability
are necessary, with purse strings loosened only for
pilot programs. It is critical that any new program
be thoroughly tested before another full-scale
assault on poverty is made.

17-35. Zimlich, Norm, and Linda A. Wilcox. "Reworking
Welfare: The States are Leading the
Nation Toward Comprehensive Reform."
Public Welfare 46 (Fall 1988): 6-18.

Current recommendations for welfare
reform are based largely on state programs and
proposals, which are not federally mandated.
Maine is promoting both jobs for low-income
people and economic development; businesses

value the wage subsidies and the tax credits and offered no resistance to the requirement that jobs be targeted to low-income people.

18 Family Policy

Many critics argue that changes in the present welfare system are not enough to end poverty among women and children. They argue that the United States must adopt family-oriented policies. In Women and Children Last: The Plight of Poor Women in Affluent America (Viking, 1986), Ruth Sidel writes, "The United States must recognize, as have Sweden and so many other industrialized countries, that the society must provide a humane environment in which people can live, work, thrive and raise their children." (p. 191)

Sidel and others point to the support for mothers and children found in many Scandinavian countries as examples of sound family policy. Unlike the Reaganites' emphasis on traditional family values and view of the male-headed, stay-at-home mother as the norm, such a policy would emphasize maternal and child health. An American family policy might include maternity and child-care leave; health care--including family planning, prenatal care, and care for children; children or family allowances; affordable accessible day care; and child-support enforcement. To such a policy, Barbara Bergman would add a job program for single parents to train them for better-paying jobs. She argues that "[a] policy package that promised government-sponsored child care, lower welfare budgets, greater independence of single mothers, and lowered poverty levels should be saleable to the American people." ("A Workable Family Policy," Dissent 35 [Winter 1988]: 88-93.)

18-1. Bergmann, Barbara R. "A Workable Family
      Policy." <u>Dissent</u> 35 (Winter 1988): 88-93.

      Families with children are struggling
today in America. The social agenda should
promote quality child care, replace welfare with a
system of guaranteed payments for children's
expenses, and include a program of helping single
parents get good jobs. Since most single parents
are women, many of them black and Hispanic,
they suffer race and sex discrimination in
employment. Apprenticeship programs, training,
job creation, and affirmative action are needed to
get single mothers into relatively well-paying jobs.
An economy committed to low unemployment and
a more liberalized version of unemployment
insurance would keep a high percentage of single
parents out of poverty.

18-2. <u>The Common Good</u>. Ford Foundation. Project on
      Social Welfare and the American Future.
      New York: Ford Foundation, 1989.

      Findings and policy recommendations of
the Executive Panel of the Project on Social
Welfare and the American Future. The panel
took a life-cycle approach, beginning with the
need for prenatal care and continuing through
retirement. The policy recommendations
emphasize the "need for a mixture of public-
(including federal, state, and local governments)
and private-sector involvement as well as
individual responsibility." Policy recommendations
directly affecting women include universal access
to prenatal care, child-care subsidies for lower-
income families, programs to encourage teenagers
not to become pregnant, and extension of
Medicaid coverage to the working poor.

18-3. Folbre, Nancy. "Whither Families: Towards a
Socialist-Feminist Family Policy."
Socialist Review 18 (1988): 57-75.

Feminists have gained rights as
individuals at the expense of the traditional
patriarchal family, a development which has had
both positive and negative effects on women and
children. Feminists need to offer strategies for
strengthening the positive aspects of family life
and to pursue reforms of government policy at all
levels. The state has to recognize not only
families based on biological kinship and legal
contracts (adoption, marriage) but also chosen
families, e.g., homosexual marriages, and allow the
extension of family-related benefits such as social
security. Child-support enforcement is necessary.
A family allowance program, similar to those in
Western European countries, should be provided
as a substitute for tax subsidies and welfare, and
supplemented by job training and child-care
programs.

18-4. Glazer, Nathan. The Limits of Social Policy.
Cambridge, MA: Harvard University
Press, 1988.

Without ever having reached European
levels, the American welfare state began to retreat
under President Carter; the process accelerated
under President Reagan. America has never
taxed as much nor spent as much as Europe for
social purposes, except in caring for the aged.
Compared to other industrialized nations, the U.S.
spends less on welfare and has a less complete
system of protection, but does have a well-
developed welfare system, and a large poor and
problem-making population. Despite the costs in
social disorder, Americans choose not to have a
national social policy.

18-5. Kelly, Robert F. "Poverty, the Family, and Public Policy: Historical Interpretations and a Reflection on the Future." In Families and Economic Distress: Coping Strategies and Social Policy, pp. 261-284. Edited by Patricia Voydanoff and Linda C. Majka. Newbury Park, CA: Sage Publications, 1988.

Kelly discusses three models that characterize policy responses to poverty and the family. The first, the laissez-faire model, emphasizes individual achievement and free markets, relies on private charity, and attempts to distinguish between the deserving and the undeserving poor. The clinical model focuses on individual rather than structural sources of poverty and emphasizes in-kind transfers and services rather than cash transfers. The family-support model emphasizes the family rather than the individual and stresses income and employment support. Kelly believes that the structural transformation of the American economy and the growth of the urban underclass offer challenges to each model. He proposes a supported work program that would both guarantee and require work of poor families.

18-6. Moynihan, Daniel Patrick. "The Family and the Nation, 1965-1986." America, March 22, 1986, pp. 221-227.

Senator Moynihan reviews his article written 21 years ago for the same periodical and finds that he was prophetic. He points out that, although the Reagan Administration touts the rise in individual income, family income has declined. Median family income for white families in 1984 was $26,394, for blacks $15,432. Moynihan emphasizes the need for a national family policy as the cornerstone for future social legislation. Such a policy need only declare that the government will promote the stability and well-being of the American family.

AUTHOR INDEX

SUBJECT INDEX

AFDC (Aid to Families
with Dependent
Children) 2-32, 2-33,
3-9, 3-31, 4-12, 9-21,
12-1, 16-2, 16-3,
16-36, 17-14, 17-17,
17-18
black women 3-23,
10-43
female-headed families
16-15, 16-22, 17-24
teenage mothers 13-4,
13-23
see also Welfare

AFSCME v. Washington
8-16, 8-18, 8-19
AIDS
black women 14-10
children 14-27, 14-28,
14-30
Hispanic women 14-1,
14-10
Abortion
Medicare and
Medicaid 14-13
see also Reproductive
health
Acquired Immune
Deficiency Syndrome
see AIDS
Affirmative action 8-7

Aid to Families with
Dependent Children
see AFDC
Albany, New York
homeless women and
children 15-6
Alimony 3-25, 5-18
Appalachia 1-4, 2-30

Behavioral dependency
16-32, 17-15, 17-26
Bibliography
feminization of poverty
2-18
Black children 4-9, 4-11,
10-12, 10-4
Black men
employment 10-8,
10-32, 10-37
Black women
see Chapter 10
AFDC 3-23, 10-43
AIDS 14-10
employment 3 23, 7-6,
7-14, 10-18, 10-19,
10-21, 10-22, 10-42
female-headed families
10-9, 10-10, 10-11,
10-12, 10-20, 10-30,
10-32, 10-39

311